Seven Stones

A PORTRAIT OF ARTHUR ERICKSON, ARCHITECT

by Edith Iglauer

HARBOUR PUBLISHING / UNIVERSITY OF WASHINGTON PRESS

Seven Stones
Copyright © 1981 Edith Iglauer

Published by

Harbour Publishing
Box 219 Madeira Park
British Columbia V0N 2H0 (Canada)

University of Washington Press
4045 Brooklyn Avenue East
Seattle, WA. 98105 (USA)

Design: James Bradburne
Typesetting and Layout: Scriveners' Publication Trades
Vancouver, Canada

Printed and bound by Friesen Printers

A portion of the text appeared in *The New Yorker* © 1979 *The New Yorker*. Permission to reprint is gratefully acknowledged.

Drawings: pages 18, 39, 41, 43, 52, 58, 92, 102, 109, Arthur Erickson.

Portrait of Arthur Erickson: Burton Silverman

Printed and bound in Canada

PHOTO CREDITS: Applied Photography, 52, 53; Clayton Bailey, back jacket, 87 bottom, 88; Dick Busher, 56, 100; John Evans, 41 bottom; Arthur Erickson, 57, 58, 61; John Fulker, 28, 69, 118; Frank Grant, 16; Art Hupy, 66 bottom; Orion Press, front jacket, 48,49; Max Sauer, 76; Simon Scott, 1, 8, 11, 13, 21, 24, 25 top, 27, 29, 32, 34 top, 36, 41 top, 44 right, 45, 50 bottom, 66 top, 67, 70, 72, 114, 115, 117; Ezra Stoller, 4-5, 23, 26, 106, 107, 108, 109; Roy Scully, 31, 34 bottom; Wayne Thom, 110.
All photos not listed above: courtesy Arthur Erickson Associates.

Overleaf:
Vancouver Civic
Centre, Vancouver
(1973)

Canadian Cataloguing in Publication Data

Iglauer, Edith
  Seven Stones
  includes index
  ISBN 0-920080-13-8
  1. Erickson, Arthur, 1924-   2. Architect—British Columbia—Biography   1. Title

NA 749.E74139   720'.924   C81-091285-6

Library of Congress Cataloguing in Publication Data

Iglauer, Edith.
  Seven Stones.
  includes index
  1. Erickson, Arthur, 1924- . I. Title.
NA749.E74T34 720'.92'4   81-13154
ISBN 0-295-95882-0 (University of Wash. Press)
AACR2

For

Jacqueline Bernstein

and

William and Emily Maxwell

ACKNOWLEDGEMENT

Part of *Seven Stones* was written on a fishing boat, the *Morekelp,* while I was trolling for salmon along the coast of British Columbia with my late husband, John Daly. Or rather, he fished and I wrote. I am thankful for that happy collaboration.

A special note of gratitude to William Shawn, editor of *The New Yorker Magazine* to whom I first presented the idea of writing about Arthur Erickson; to Howard White, of Harbour Publishing, who insisted that I explore that subject further, so we could make this book; and to the many others who encouraged me, especially Geoff and Margaret Andrew.

Simon Fraser University, Burnaby, B.C. (1963). View of mall.

Overleaf: Academic quad, SFU.

In the summer of 1968 my sons and I visited the Canadian Northwest for the first time, with vague notions, like most Americans have, of immersing ourselves in spectacular scenery, especially in British Columbia. As we were departing from the United States a friend said, "When you get to Vancouver, don't miss Simon Fraser University!"

And so on a fine August day we rented a car in Vancouver, drove up a small mountain at the edge of the city, and on its summit we found Simon Fraser University. Standing on that mountaintop, at the entrance to the great mall of the university, frosty white peaks to our right, the gleam of the Pacific Ocean far below to our left, the light piping sound of a Mozart sonata floating in the air from the flute of an unseen student, we found ourselves looking down a dazzling series of stairs and landings where sunlight and shadow added design within design, stairs flowing to levels of space flowing into the lengthy sweep of the mall, half covered by a long roof of truss-supported glass that continued into sunny distance beyond our vision—the whole suggesting by its grace and freshness such creative vitality that we had to know at once who the architect was. The university's information center gave us our answer: Arthur Erickson.

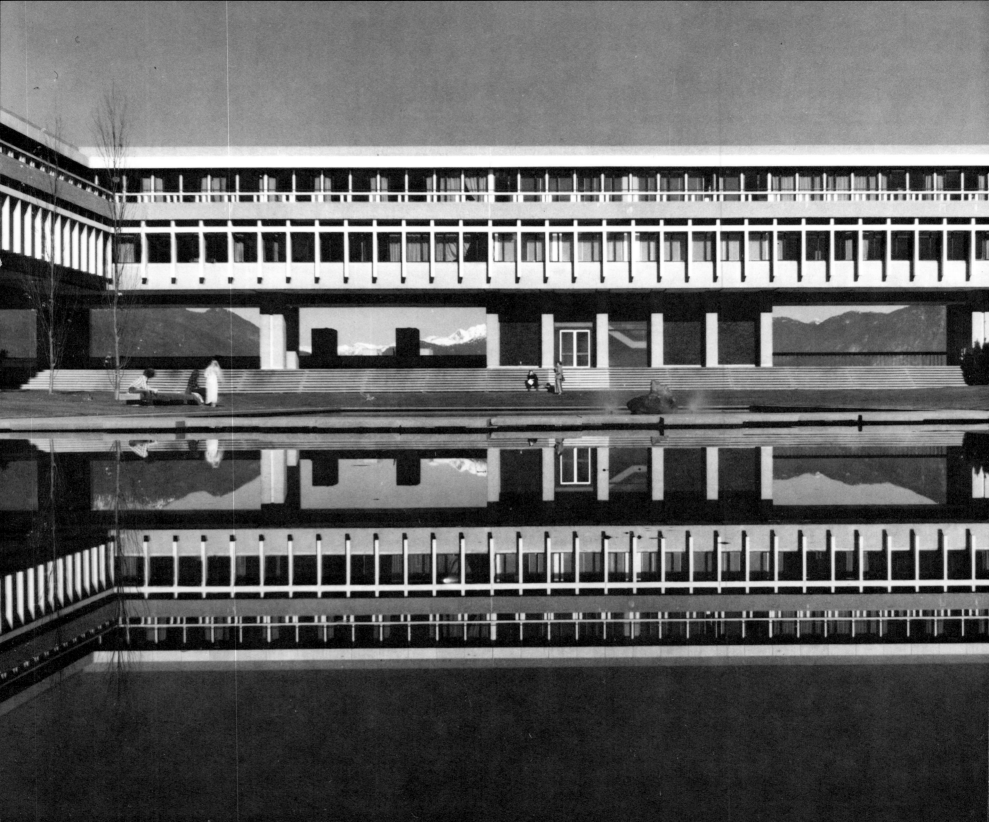

Introduction

Simon Fraser University, completed in 1965, was the first Erickson design to catch the world's attention—a dramatic, low-lying concrete megastructure that hugs the ridged summit of Burnaby Mountain, against the scenic backdrop of snow-covered peaks which it shares with Vancouver. Tagged "the instant university," because it was conceived and completed in two years by Erickson and his then partner, Geoffrey Massey, working with four other firms, Simon Fraser is faintly reminiscent at a distance of a Greek acropolis, and has a beauty that has prompted another Canadian architect, Bruno Freschi, to predict that it will make an elegant ruin.

In 1970, the *New York Times* critic Ada Louise Huxtable made a special pilgrimage to Simon Fraser and declared it a "remarkably impressive experiment in academic architecture" of "edifying brilliance." Viewing the several university buildings as one structure, she pronounced the unifying device, the glass-roofed central mall a quarter of a mile long, "one of the more magnificent socio-architectural spaces of recent years."

Although Arthur Erickson has since adorned the North American landscape with some of its most admired architecture and is engaged in designing multi-block complexes in Vancouver, Toronto, Seattle, Los Angeles and the Middle East, he has only recently become well known outside Canada.

"Why?" I asked Philip Johnson, *grand seigneur* of American architects. "It's a question of acceptance," Johnson replied. "Arthur Erickson isn't one of the smart young men—he's not their generation—but he is by far the greatest architect in Canada, and may be the greatest on this continent. However, Erickson's a Western architect and what's worse, he's in British Columbia, which is a province of a province to us.'' Turning to the subject of Simon Fraser University, he said, ''In architecture, there is always a problem we are trying to solve. In the twenties and the fifties, it was the skyscraper. In the sixties, we expressed our interest in new campuses, and Simon Fraser was the best. Its spatial arrangements are incredible. A centering device is not new —the Greeks had their temples, the Romans their circuses, and in medieval times it was the church—but the vastness of the covered mall at Simon Fraser University is the best symbolic central device for a campus I know of anyplace.''

Paul Rudolph, former chairman of Yale University's Department of Architecture and today an eminent New York architect, regards Erickson as Canada's best architect. ''Erickson's work is very very good indeed,'' he says. ''He's one of the most distinguished architects living.''

Erickson, sometimes in partnership and sometimes alone, has designed and built apartment houses, schools, office buildings, banks, museums, three prize-winning international fair structures, a Sikh temple, a plastic swimming-pool cabana, a visitors' pavilion made of recycled newspapers for the 1976 United Nations Habitat Conference in Vancouver, two subway stations in Toronto and more private houses than he can remember. His house designs range from a dramatic combination residence-and-museum for a wealthy

New Massey Hall, Toronto (1976). Model photograph showing ceiling.

''All great opera houses have ceilings worth looking up at when you're bored.''
—Erickson

Opposite: Habitat Pavilion, Vancouver (1977). Underside of papier-mache canopy showing hand-painted panels.

12

Waterfront Centre, Vancouver (1980). Model photograph.

"One of the most moving memories I have from my childhood is going down to watch the cruise ships— mostly the Empress boats from India and China, coming or going. They always had a brass band and coloured streamers. These were great occasions, when people left or returned from such mysterious lands. I want to express that gateway."
—Erickson

Harbour Steps, Seattle (1980) Model photograph of mixed housing, commercial, office and shopping complex located in run-down part of Seattle waterfront with broad, shop-lined flight of steps and fountains as central element.

"The real problem was to provide a residential environment that would get people to start living downtown again. It is a wonderful site, but next to a waterfront freeway that was one of Seattle's great mistakes."
—Erickson

Seattle lumber family, the Bagley Wrights, and their collection of modern art, to a rustic island dwelling off the British Columbia coast for rock musician Boz Scaggs, which Erickson has described as a "rudimentary living, whole-earth-catalogue-type house design" that collects its own rain water for household use and has a windmill. Larger projects vary from single buildings like his handsome, unorthodox Museum of Anthropology at the University of British Columbia, to the Bank of Canada in Ottawa, and a pharmaceutical research plant adjoining England's Cambridge University. His mixed-use complexes include the dramatic new Massey Concert Hall, park and office buildings in Toronto; the Harbor Steps project combining apartments, office towers, a hotel and pedestrian mall in Seattle; the colossal development in the Bunker Hill district of Los Angeles; an assortment of universities, towns and shopping centres in the Middle East; a housing project and urban study for Victoria's Songhees Peninsula; a hotel and office buildings on Vancouver's waterfront; and his most conspicuous work in Vancouver, the Courthouse-Robson Square Civic Centre.

In that three-block project he has introduced indoor and outdoor gardens with orange trees and flowering shrubs, three waterfalls and a miniature forest. Facilities include shops, a small cinema, restaurants, an ice-skating rink that converts to roller-skating in the summer and an exhibition hall-conference centre next to provincial offices that are partly submerged below the street. The apex of the project is a radical new courthouse with a sloping block-long glass roof. Facing the courthouse at the opposite end of the site is the old courthouse, a graceful building designed in 1910 by Francis Rattenbury, whose architecture can also be viewed at the Empress Hotel and the Parliament Buildings in Victoria. Erickson has revamped the old Vancouver landmark into the city's new art gallery, and has retained its neo-classical style without making it seem out of place.

The complex, which cost about a hundred million dollars to build, has transformed downtown life in British Columbia's largest city. When it opened, the *New York Times* again sent its architecture critic to take a look. This time it was Paul Goldberger, who arrived in late November, 1979, and wrote, "The new courthouse . . . is clearly the centerpiece of downtown . . . despite the fact that it has no classical columns, no formal portico, and no marble lobby, the way most courthouses that stand as symbols do. Moreover, the new Law Courts . . . is just seven storeys high, making it dwarfed by many of the city's gleaming new skyscrapers. The court building manages to be the commanding presence of downtown Vancouver nonetheless."

Goldberger was dubious about subsurface areas and wished for a bit less concrete and more greenery above, but he pronounced Robson Square "a piece of architecture; design has been permitted to play a role here that it rarely achieves in purely commercial ventures," with the courthouse the real triumph. "Mr. Erickson has managed to achieve grandeur without resorting to literal reuse of the past and without indulging in the austerity that makes so

15

Napp Pharmaceutical Laboratories, Cambridge, England (1979). Model Photo.

"It's a factory, warehouse, and research facility and therefore it is paramount to have every surface impervious to corrosion and easily cleanable. Mirrored glass also gives a beautiful, ambient light for working, in the big spaces."
—Erickson

Spadina Quay, Toronto (1981). Residential Complex on the downtown harbourfront. Model photo.

"The whole shape of four buildings, three residential and one office, of concrete and glass, plus an existing warehouse, must fit into a predetermined envelope, with curved corners and a ground arcade, terraced back, so that almost everyone gets an exposed terrace and waterfront view. Very difficult restrictions!"

New Massey Hall Complex, Toronto (1976). Ten acre site known as "Downtown West" with the concert hall occupying 2.5 acres in the foreground and three-acre Massey Hall Park in the middle flanked by three office buildings.
Model photo.

Opposite: California Centre, Bunker Hill, Los Angeles (1980).

"A billion-dollar project on the last big piece of undeveloped land in downtown Los Angeles. We won the competition because they only asked for a museum and small park as amenities to a big commercial-residential complex, but we gave so much more. We integrated the museum with a system of linear parks, a performing and cinematic centre, music, dance, dining, shopping—we provided a whole smorgasbord of ideas all interrelated and treated as part of the culture. A lot of these ideas were expanded from ideas we developed for Robson Square in Vancouver."
—Bing Thom

many modern public buildings so forbidding," he continued. "Mr. Erickson wants symbolism and he wants warmth, and he has achieved both; his great space is not only grand, but welcoming."

Designing a complex of any size is an occupation Erickson thoroughly enjoys, even though most are so huge that he must join together with a consortium of other architects and engineers to minimize the financial risk for any single office. So long as he is in charge of the master plan and can design the buildings for which he is directly responsible he is happy.

The project on Bunker Hill in Los Angeles is the largest job of design Erickson has had in North America. It is ten times the size of Vancouver's Civic Centre, and is expected to take eight to ten years to complete. Saudi Arabia has sought Erickson's designing talents for several projected architectural concepts: the King Abdul Aziz University for twenty thousand students, which will cost several billion dollars and take at least seven years to build; the King Faisal Air Force Academy for fifteen hundred students; a private Islamic University for eighteen thousand students in Medina; and project management of a new Ministry of Foreign Affairs complex to be built at Riyadh.

In the early nineteen-sixties Arthur Erickson, then a young university professor teaching architecture, with no experience in building anything bigger than a house, was catapulted into the orbit of important architects with one significant design—for Simon Fraser University. It was a comforting

16

affirmation of the imaginative approach to massive contemporary building; he challenged mass with structures that aimed to please the eye and the spirit. In the late sixties and seventies, he continued to apply this design philosophy with success; and in the eighties Erickson has become one of the world's outstanding architects.

I am not an architectural critic or authority but an ordinary viewer of buildings who has had a helpless admiration for architectural excellence ever since I first looked up from the street and noticed the differences in structures. The interest which inspired this book began with that moment of sunshiny delight, looking down the great mall of Simon Fraser University in the summer of 1968.

I like to think I am writing not so much about architecture as about the mind of an architect. Viewing Erickson's buildings, I became increasingly curious about the mind that could inspire so many remarkable and varied designs. I especially wanted to know how Erickson manages to protect the fragile creative process from the terrible pressures of the world he must inhabit as a successful architect.

Boz Scaggs House, Lasqueti Island, B.C. (1980).

"He [Scaggs] has a nice sense of the rudimentary living he wants in his house, having been to Japan. Drinking water is gathered from the roof, washing water from the courtyard, with a common bathhouse. Everything is to be built from trees on the island, with local stone for the floors."
—Erickson

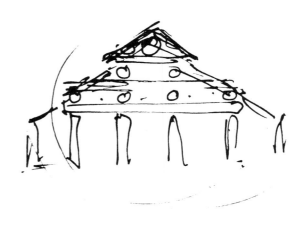

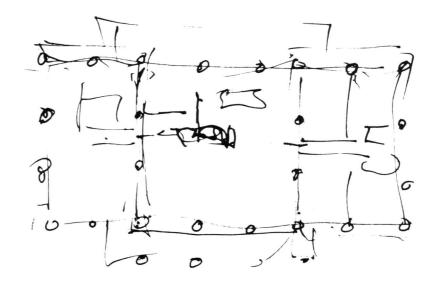

Erickson, a witty, semi-mystical, not at all humble man in his mid-fifties, says, "Where I am or what I am is no concern of mine. I am concerned with what our civilization is all about, and expressing this in buildings. Everything I do, everything I see is through architecture. It has given me a vehicle for looking at the world. I am not involved in the aesthetics of architecture or interested in design as such. I'm interested in what buildings can do beyond what they look like, and how they can affect whole areas and people's lives. I have never done a building where I didn't at least attempt to see it in a new philosophical or social way. I could have asked questions in any field, but I am doing it through my buildings. What panics me is how little time I have. Now I want to build with all details suppressed, to make what I build look as if it had just

happened—as if there was nothing studied, no labour or art involved. Architecture is no different from any other art process. It is like poetry, in which you compress everything into a few words. To achieve that economy takes a lifetime."

A colleague who was asked to classify Erickson's architecture exclaimed, "Why, Arthur doesn't even follow himself!" Erickson's architectural style has been defined as lyrical, cool, daring, romantic, monumental, contemporary, classical, derivative, original, neo-Inca, timeless, modern—and sometimes as just breathtakingly beautiful. There are recognizable Erickson devices: strong horizontals; wooden lattices to soften solid wall mass; high fences or plantings for privacy; skylights; flooded roofs or ground pools to catch reflections; the illusion of infinity; a mound of earth

Bagley Wright House, Seattle (1977).

somewhere outside (which Erickson calls "my signature"). But by and large his most consistent trait is inconsistency, professionally and personally. This has produced a deliberate method of living which he thrives on, and which Geoffrey Massey has described as "consistent chaos."

Erickson says that designing space for human beings to use—preferably clusters of buildings and the land and water around them—occupies almost all his conscious moments, and he believes that it absorbs an even higher percentage of his unconscious, or what he refers to as his superconscious, thoughts. In the Canadian *Who's Who,* he once listed architecture and travelling as his "recreations" and he has not stayed more than ten days in one place since 1965. Travelling enables him to check up on every type of building constructed by civilized man, and possibly by earlier human species, going back to the Paleolithic era. "North America is in a very primitive stage, because culture takes hundreds of years to evolve," Erickson has said. "I am fortunate that I can stand in Canada, a country without a culture, and look at the world. When I am given a project such as a university or a courthouse or a museum, I can detach myself from patterns of learning about that type of structure in North America, because I know the solutions at Oxford, at the El Azhar mosque in Cairo, or at a temple in Thailand. I can say, 'What is its essence? How can I extract something pertinent for today?'"

Many of Erickson's commissions are won in competition, and he has lost count of the awards and medals he has acquired—three or four dozen. In 1975 he received the Auguste Perret Award (named for an early Parisian researcher into reinforced concrete), that is presented every three years by the International Union of Architects. In 1978 the American Institute of Architects, whose Hawaii chapter had previously given him an award for "singular individuality and excellence in design," made him an Honorary Fellow, and in the spring of 1979 he became the first Canadian to receive the most distinguished American honour in landscape design, the President's Award from the American Society of Landscape Architects.

A prize of fifty thousand dollars and a gold medal was given him by the Royal Bank of Canada in 1971. This is a distinction conferred on one Canadian annually for contributions "to human welfare and the common good" and earlier recipients include the late brain surgeon Dr. Wilder Penfield and novelist Morley Callaghan.

The essence of Erickson's consistent inconsistency was expressed in the speech he made to the Canadian business establishment at the sumptuous banquet held in his honour on the occasion of the Royal Bank award. He is a sophisticated observer of the power structure, who knows where the vast sums must come from to make an architect's designs materialize. Yet he scolded the assembled businessmen for the "ruthless economic competition" in North American cities, which expresses itself in streets that are "wastelands of parked cars . . . grim, sunless spaces between towering edifices . . . showing our priorities for

Museum of Anthropology, University of British Columbia (1972). Interior of great hall showing continuous plexiglass skylights.

"When I saw those plexiglass details I almost fainted. They are beyond what one could expect as feasible. Only Arthur would have the nerve to do it. Some poor bastard may spend the next couple of years figuring out how to solve the leaks, but this way it's almost as if it's open to the sky, as if all barriers disappear."
—Geoffrey Massey

South-East Sector School, Vancouver (1972). Skylight over the main classroom

"In my school you come out into this central area under a skylight for whatever the children do together, for all their general school activities. There are no partitions between the classrooms and the central area. The idea was to have a completely open school; one huge classroom that appears to be open to the sky."
—Erickson

Robson Square, Vancouver (1973) Detail of concrete stairs, Media Centre.

"Concrete is as noble a material as limestone. There is no paint to mar its surface or contrasting materials to detract from its inherent beauty. As in all serious architecture, the structural material is consistent, pervasive, and unadorned."
—Erickson

Eppich House, Vancouver, 1974. Concrete staircase.

"I don't think concrete is beautiful per se, but I think if one accepts it as the building stone of our century one can find beautiful qualities in it—its earthiness, its mass, its traces of how it's made—I really do like it."
—Erickson

services, roadways and real estate." He defined the bulldozer as the "symbol of North America." He asked for a shift of "mind set"—the term he uses for rigid values that control the future development of ideas—away from "aggressive independence and self-sufficient individuality" and toward a "balance between economic profit and social well-being." He posed the question "Should not the land come under public ownership so that the ultimate control is in the public's hands?"

As a speaker, Erickson has been described as a spellbinder. An architect's wife has recalled, "I once heard Arthur give a speech on brutalism in architecture to a meeting of architects, with a seraphic smile on his face, in that beautiful speaking voice of his. I couldn't help feeling that Arthur could get things done in any society, because he is quite tough, despite that smile. I wouldn't want to cross him!" Erickson ordinarily accepts one or two carefully selected speaking invitations a year, from sources that will enable him, in his words, "to tell the very ones who should be told" what his views are. He made Vancouver newspaper headlines with a speech to the Men's Canadian Club on May 28, 1976 urging that, since British Columbia's arable land is scarce, the land in the Fraser Valley be held by the government and reserved for food production, with buildings or settlements "relegated to the higher slopes." He said, "One needn't own land—that is another nineteenth-century illusion we must dispose of—if we can lease it for whatever length of time is necessary to accomplish our purpose. After all, look at the centre of London."

At the 1974 International Congress of Architecture in Iran, he pleaded with Third World countries to preserve their own cultures, to avoid the Western solution of freeways and high rises—"all the trashy neon and plastic glitter"—and added that what the West has "thrown on the waters of the world drifts back to us on a tide of cultural pollution appalling to behold." In 1975 at a meeting of the International Union of Architects in Madrid, he pronounced Western architectural techniques "stifling" and begged the assembled architects to adopt urban forms consistent with their own diverse cultures rather than simply to follow the lead of the West. He recommended that they suspend rational thought to achieve "a floating, unselective frame of mind . . . in order to receive information from all sources unconditionally." To put it in Zen terms, he said, "it is only the empty vessel that can be filled."

Erickson feels that differences between the architecture of the East and that of the West are a result of opposing attitudes toward man's importance: in the West, man is at the centre of everything, while Eastern concepts make him a part of the larger schemes of nature. At a meeting of the Institute of Canadian Bankers in 1972 Erickson compared the imposition by tourists from the West of their own values on other cultures to "an infectious disease decimating whatever values existed before." Their egocentricity, he said, makes them "incapable of measuring things except in their own terms;" they regard ancient living cultures as "undeveloped" and their current practitioners as "non-

Macmillan Bloedel Building, Vancouver (1969).

"In Macmillan Bloedel I was very conscious of bringing out the beauty of the concrete and did some things which are not considered good concrete practice. For example, it's not wise to pour concrete to have sharp corners because they break off when you strip the forms. At MB all the corners are sharp because I felt that breaking off edges would enhance rather than detract. The use of concrete was so simple in that building: the variations that occurred in the making provide the interest."
—Erickson

achievers." After this warmup he attacked the World Bank specifically, for funding a "multi-storeyed, monster" hotel in Afghanistan, in "one of the most beautiful valleys in the world" and a three-thousand-room hotel development in Bali, "whose impact on that island will be terminal." He said, "You as bankers, cannot afford to be concerned with only the economic aspects of projects that you finance. There may be serious implications . . . which at some future time may even be considered crimes against mankind."

Commenting later on his address to the bankers, he remarked, "I felt that it had to be said, but I expected a disaster and was amazed at the applause." He noted that the bankers published this speech in their journal and gave it their award for the best talk of 1972.

In October, 1978, at the World Congress of the International Union of Architects in Mexico City, he attacked tourism again as an industry that has "gone wild," comparing package tours to plagues of locusts that "arrive, destroy, and leave conscienceless from the havoc they have wreaked." Referring again to the new hotels in Bali and Afghanistan, he continued, "Architects and international agencies have conspired in this . . . desecration," producing "overcrowding and sleazy developments . . . . As the number of empty or deteriorating hotels has increased, the tourist agencies have looked elsewhere for a virgin place ripe for raping . . . . In America, a new kind of anonymous city was born—Anywhere, U.S.A.—to spread everywhere in the late sixties and seventies as unchallengeable American expertise

25

Yorkdale Subway Station, Toronto (1977). Interior of ceiling vault.

"We got an artist, Michael Hayden, to create a light sculpture that runs the whole length of the station, and pulsates as the train comes in, with a whole spectrum of colour. In architecture, art should not just be an ornament."
—Erickson

Yorkdale Subway Station, Toronto (1977).

Opposite: Royal Bank of Canada Headquarters, Ottawa (1976)

Macmillan Bloedel Building, Vancouver (1969)

"This company deals with a rugged resource and I wanted a no-nonsense building. I wanted to go to the simplest form of construction, the bearing wall, where your exterior wall carries the weight of the building all the way up. It's the opposite of the curtain wall where your weight is carried on columns and your exterior wall is very light."
—Erickson

became in universal demand, giving birth to Anywhere, The World."

He said afterward, "The audiences I speak to are the people with the power to make changes. You don't want to flatter if things are not as they should be. I repeat and repeat and repeat in my speeches. All one can hope is that what I say will have some meaning to someone and may influence his life and, through his, influence someone else's. I am completely apolitical, but I am pro people. If I can get away with what I say in the circles I speak in, it's because I am considered a member of their group. It is important to upset them."

Erickson was born in Vancouver and spent his first twenty years there. It is still his home and his headquarters, though he commutes weekly two thousand seventy-eight air miles east to a second office he maintains in Toronto, when he isn't journeying elsewhere. He ascribes to his native British Columbia, with its amiably wet climate and extravagant amount of beautiful scenery, his inability to conceive of a building apart from its setting. Most of his projects were in this western area until the mid-seventies when he began working his way east and into acceptance as an international architect. He uses wood, the principal natural resource of his province, in his structures the way an artist applies paint to a canvas. As a youth Erickson composed poetry and painted. When he was sixteen his sketches and paintings received public recognition, and he seriously considered becoming a painter. Today he approaches architecture with a poet's rhythm and a painter's vision. In a large, lavishly illustrated book, *The Architecture of Arthur Erickson,* which was published in 1975, he wrote that, for him, architecture's vital components are part of a single creative process taking into account site, light, cadence, space and the people who will use the building. His richest source of inspiration he described as "the 'dialogue' between a building and its setting," adding that "the local light will eventually determine the architectural style." The cadence he has since explained as the rhythm set off by the spatial and structural system, stairs, landings and window openings that complement one another through the building. He wrote then that he is motivated by space the way a musician is inspired by sound or a sculptor by form.

A Vancouver journalist named Mary McAlpine, who is a lifelong friend of Erickson's, once remarked that she would be afraid to have him design a house for her (although since then she has courageously added an Erickson-designed study, with a fireplace and a solarium with a vaulted roof, along one side of her residence). "His houses reflect the whole person," she said. "He finds the secret part of a person that isn't showing." For the headquarters in Vancouver of MacMillan Bloedel, the giant lumber concern, he designed a twin-towered concrete structure of monolithic appearance which tapers as it rises, like a tree trunk, and has deep-set, square windows. It was described in *Architectural Record* as having an "elegant leanness," but it is often referred to as Fort MacMillan. To such comments, Erickson responds serenely, "My most Doric building. What I wanted

27

Biological Sciences Building, University of Victoria, Victoria (1970)
"Any laboratory has to have heavy air equipment, so we put all the air handling equipment and the exhaust, which is very complicated, on top. That's the reason for those box beams on the roof."
—Erickson

Sikh Temple, Vancouver (1969)

Smith House, Vancouver (1964)

"The relationship between building and site should be so intimate that a 'dialogue' seems to be established between the two—a play of counterpoint between land shape and building form. There should be no back or side or front, no less attractive aspect of the house, but all parts should have an equally vital relationship with the site."

—Erickson

Catton House, Vancouver (1967)

"The budget was very limited and we met it—eighteen or nineteen dollars a square foot, damned good for an architect designed house."

—Nick Milkovich, project architect

to express *was* mass." In 1974 he designed a coldly classic modern showplace in Vancouver—referred to as the Eppich house, after its owner, a German-Canadian manufacturer of metal parts and machines—and it won Erickson an award from *Architectural Record*: his third from that magazine for the design of a house. In a previous prize-winning house, this one for his intimate Vancouver friends Gordon and Marion Smith, both artists, he used the same horizontals and verticals in wood that in the Eppich house were transposed into concrete. The Smith house was also in a woodland setting, and he used similar sliding glass walls to integrate nature into the design, but the effect here is warm and intimate.

"I have often thought that I was more of a landscape designer than an architect," Erickson wrote in his book. "I tend to take a structural approach to landscape and a landscape approach to architecture . . . . In my own garden, for example, it was only after I had buried what had been an English border garden beneath a high mound of earth that I recognized that the character of the site was that of a forest clearing."

The forest clearing that Erickson created for his home is on a sixty-six-by-one-hundred-and-twenty-foot city lot in a neighbourhood of small houses fronted with patches of lawn. His house, however, has a high cedar fence around it and, like the majority of the dwellings he has designed for others, is almost invisible from the street. Bushes and trees peer enticingly over the fence, and an odd-shaped roof with skylights is barely discernible through the foliage. Two garages and a lean-to were at the back of the lot when Erickson bought it, in 1957, for eleven thousand dollars. The previous owner had lived in one garage and the lean-to, reserving the second garage for a car. Erickson doesn't own a car; he ordinarily rents cars, and uses a lane at his back door for parking—a practice that is frowned upon by the city, as are high fences. His house now consists of the original garages and the lean-to, which has become part of the small, skylit connective structure, containing the bathroom and kitchen: a total area of twelve hundred square feet. His living room has the unmistakable rectangular dimensions of a narrow, one-car garage, and so does his bedroom-study, but in each the wall facing the garden has been replaced by sliding glass.

The visitor to Erickson's house, upon opening a gate in the fence, enters a magical realm of trees, bushes and wild grasses surrounding a small body of water that appears to be a lake; at the far end of this garden there is a small mountain. The lake is actually an artfully placed pond deep enough to contain fish and the mountain is an eight-foot mound of earth, but illusion is everywhere: spacious, lovely country landscape continuing into the beyond. From the gate the visitor follows stepping stones through this sylvan scene, crosses a wooden deck and steps down to a brick patio, where a glass door set into an off-white travertine-marble wall appears to arrive at the visitor's feet rather than the other way around, or so it seemed one day when I visited Erickson. I could see him through the glass, coming to the door with a rapid, lithe step: slim, of medium height, casually dressed in tan

29

Eppich House, Vancouver (1974)

"This property was a garbage dump . . . We did the landscape plan first and then designed the house . . . on top of the garbage dump, so you don't see it. It was a very simple and logical decision . . .
It was my first concrete house. These people were Europeans and they didn't like wood houses because of fire and . . . had been used to masonry . . . so I was delighted to use concrete."
—Erickson

slacks, a black-and-white checked sports shirt and a tan cardigan sweater. He has short, curly grey hair flecked with brown and some white; his eyes are a friendly blue. He has sometimes been mistaken for a dilettante because he enjoys the company of wealthy and famous people; in the East he gravitates toward the international jet set, dropping the names of members into his conversation as if their acceptance of him surprised him. He is a gifted raconteur. In Vancouver he relaxes within a small circle of artists, writers and teachers, among whom old friends predominate; or with his brother Donald —a talented writer and teacher, who is four years younger—and Donald's family, to all of whom he is devoted. In company, Erickson almost always seems to be smiling or laughing, but his outwardly easygoing nature disguises a compulsive worker who is somewhat solitary. The unsmiling Erickson has a long, serious face and determined features that all seem to be pointed: peaked hairline, aquiline nose, wide but tapered mouth and firm, pointed chin.

Erickson told me he had just returned from a business trip that took him to Toronto, New York and the Middle East, and allowed him a day of skiing in the Swiss Alps, which included glacier-hopping by helicopter—a new variation for him of the only sport besides scuba diving in which he indulges. Erickson's enthusiasms translate into verbal extravagance, some of his favourite words being "extraordinary," "spectacular," "incredible," and "absolutely." He described the experience of being dropped by a helicopter on "a little handkerchief of ice," then skiing five thousand feet to the bottom of a valley and being picked up there by the helicopter and transported to the top of another glacier to ski down as "absolutely incredible."

It was ten on a Sunday morning, and Erickson had just prepared his breakfast—a blended liquid of fresh orange juice, milk, wheat germ, vegetable protein and vitamins. He started coffee in a glittering miniature espresso machine on a teak kitchen counter, and while the coffee gurgled

and hissed we stood looking into the garden from the living room. It is a small room with a velvety carpet, low sofas around small tables and walls lined with five-inch squares of Italian suede—all a soft-beige contrast to the off-white of the drapes, travertine floors, fireplace and tabletops. Erickson used to sleep in the living room on a couch made of straw streetcar seat backs, but recently he was persuaded by Francisco Kripacz, who advises him on interiors, to adopt this more elegant simplicity and to create new sleeping arrangements in the other garage building. Except for a slim, delicately carved eighteenth-century Japanese goddess of mercy on the mantel, several small pottery pieces on clear Plexiglas shelves around the fireplace and two Oriental figures on pedestals, the art that he has collected in his travels has been consigned to teak cupboards. Simple statement extends even to the kitchen, where formerly open shelves have disappeared behind teak panels. In the bathroom, fixtures are of black porcelain, and almost invisible.

Outside, a typical Vancouver rain squall started, transforming the garden into a glistening jungle. "For years, I was going to move to a view of open water, but this place is so convenient, because I can shut it and leave," said Erickson, drinking his breakfast as he talked. "Besides, I have to have a limited, closed view, so I can withdraw into my own world. When I moved into this house, in 1957, I was teaching architecture at the University of British Columbia and collecting pottery. The things that surrounded me were more important to me. That pot is upside

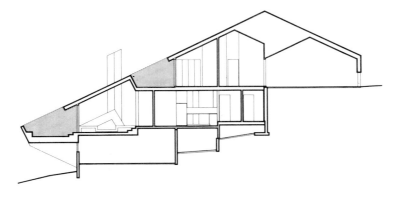

Catton House

down!'' Interrupting himself, he walked over to a shelf where a small brown square pot with a slim neck stood, broad end down. He turned its neck to the bottom, and laughed. ''It's by a well-known English potter, Hans Coper, and every second week, when my cleaning woman comes, she turns it upside down.'' He took a soft-green plate off another shelf. ''I love this piece—it's a version of Sung celadon, and I got it in the Celebes,'' he said. ''I have always been fascinated by pottery. It gives you such an intimate relationship with the person who did it.'' He ran a finger along the fluted edge, stopping at a flat spot. ''This potter made the edge with his fingers, and you can see where he had his doubts and failed to do it!'' He touched some tiny pinpricks in the middle of the plate. ''In classical pottery, there should be two fish in the centre. I don't know what this is, but it's off-centre. Imagine a Chinese potter in the outer provinces who knew of the great Sung pieces trying to duplicate one from memory on his own wheel!''

He put the plate back. ''In 1965, when I started travelling every week to Montreal to work for Expo on Canada's Man in the Community pavilion, everything changed. I loved my little house, but suddenly possessions had no importance. I realized I could live happily out of a suitcase, and didn't really need even that, and I had a freedom I had never had before. Architecturally, this house is terrible, but it serves as a refuge, a kind of decompression chamber. The nice thing about the garden is that I started it and it's been doing its own thing ever since.''

The rain stopped suddenly, and the

Overleaf:
Erickson House,
View of yard.

31

sun made a trembling attempt to enter the garden through the dripping trees. "I bought this house for its wonderful garden," he went on. "A charming Englishwoman who lived here had a white picket fence, phlox, delphiniums, lupines, Shasta daisies, a rose arbour with a strawberry-and-vegetable garden behind it and a lovely lawn. I thought the place could be self-sufficient, but the catch was that someone had to take care of all that. The second year it became like a deserted garden. It was terribly romantic, the kind of secret garden that children love—saturated with weeds but with the flowers still growing and the grass a foot high. The third year, the weeds took over entirely, so I got a bulldozer and told the operator to bury the garden, dig a hole, and make a hill high enough so I couldn't see the house across the street. I didn't have this high fence then, and I *had* to get rid of that view. Everybody in the neighbourhood thought I was excavating to build a house, and chatted with me over the picket fence, very happy to believe that they were no longer going to have a nonconformist garage dweller among them. I hired a student to line the hole with roofing paper and fill it with water, and I have never touched this pond since. I got grasses and rushes from the Fraser River, dug plants and the pine trees from the forest, put in ten different species of bamboo, the ten-foot-high zebra grass you can just see, and those very rare Himalayan rhododendrons. The dogwood, apple, pear, and plum trees are from the old garden, and I put in the persimmon tree. Then I just let the whole thing go."

How had he achieved such an impression of depth and space, I asked.

"You put as many horizontal planes, one in front of another, within your field of vision as possible," he said. "Your eye has to take in the whole series, and reads that as greater space. If you put in water, psychologically you have to cross it, and the resulting sense of remoteness extends the visual effect to another land. If I have a lavish party, I put musicians across the water, and it's as if they were playing from an island over the sea. Actually, there are twelve planes: the deck right out here, the low hedge, the brick terrace beyond the hedge, the marble slab that sticks out over the pool, the water, the edge of the rushes and grass, the gravel beach on the other side, the pine trees, the juniper that grows horizontally on the mound, the bamboo, the dogwood and fir, and those poplar trees at the fence. Everything is starved for water in the summer, but it's planned so as to keep a certain discipline. Otherwise, it would do too well the rest of the time in this wet climate. The charm of the garden is that everything has survived, because it is in its natural habitat. I have a gardener in just twice a year, and I am an observer, not an intruder. It is endlessly fascinating to see what it will produce."

The espresso machine stopped hissing, and Erickson filled two pottery mugs with coffee and added hot milk. We sat down in the kitchen on tan leather chairs at a glass table, beneath a vaulted Plexiglas skylight with green plants set along its interior rim; this overhead garden bisects the roof of the kitchen and of the bathroom, directly behind.

"My problem is raccoons," he said, taking a sip of coffee. "I had to get fish to balance the ecology of the pond, so that I would never have to clean it. Raccoons find it an ideal fishing ground, and often arrive between one and two in the morning for dessert, following raids on all the neighbourhood garbage cans. After Expo, I brought back a gorgeous carp that had been in our pavilion. It was two feet long and a pale, pale metallic gold that glistened. I released it in the pool, and the very next morning all that was left was scales, floating like gold coins. I had become quite paranoid about the raccoons, and that was the last straw. I really had thought that the carp was too big for them. I phoned the head of the Vancouver Zoo, Alan Best, and he gave me a box trap, which I baited with sardines and a bowl of milk. Then close friends who live two doors

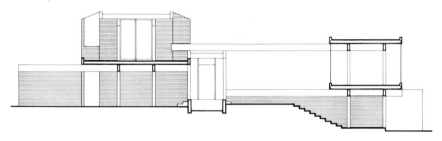

Smith House

Erickson House.

"Architecturally this house is so terrible that I would never admit to being here. In summer the garden's like a jungle. Wild heron come to feed, wild ducks come out of the pond. Once when it was half-finished I was gardening and two neighbour women looked through a hole in the old picket fence. I heard one say, 'It's a tragic story. This poor fellow started to build his house and when he dug, he struck a spring and it all turned into a swamp!'"
—Erickson

Below: Erickson House, study.

down came for drinks, and one of them said, 'You know, we've been looking for Puss for two days!' Well, a surprised Puss was all I ever caught in that trap. Alan said the next time I had raccoons I should call him even if it was two in the morning, so I did. He came right over, climbed a tree and shot one, and five police cars appeared. A neighbour had reported robbers in my garden. The next day Alan sent me two Australian black swans to keep the raccoons away. I had to get the swans a case of lettuce a day or they would have eaten everything in the garden, and they made a mud slide of my hill, because they were bored. They wanted to come in the house, and banged on the window until I let them in. Then if I shut the door they chased me out and deposited digested lettuce all over the house." He sighed. "Now I am resigned to the raccoons. I buy one hundred goldfish every summer—fish that are sold as bait for ten dollars a hundred—and usually five survive. Some fish are smarter than others."

The telephone rang, and Erickson went into his bedroom-study to answer it. The various parts of his house flow into one another, and I could see Erickson sitting and talking at a table desk strewn with books and architectural drawings. Behind him, contrasting pleasantly with the yellow Thai-silk walls, was a white bookcase, and above that was a large platform bed. A carpeted ladder led up to the bed, over which a big skylight had been cut into the sharp slant of the former garage roof. The only other furniture was a tubular chrome-and-black-pony-skin lounge chair, a classic by Le Corbusier. Erickson likes to rest in it briefly, with his

34

feet above his head, after he comes home from work and before he goes out to dinner, facing a small plant-filled conservatory between his study and the sliding glass outside wall to the garden. Erickson can step out from here into a second, smaller pool partially hidden by foliage, where he can take a relaxing soak, if he ever gets the time. Not much larger than a bathtub, it is heated and is equipped with an electric whirlpool.

Erickson returned to the kitchen, resuming the conversation before he sat down again. "The original picket fence broke, and ten years ago I put up a seven-foot wooden fence," he said. "A city regulation limited fence height to four feet, and when the neighbours objected I cut it down to six. The woman across the street still complained, so I had to apply for a variance at a meeting of the City Council. I am sorry to say I lost my cool. Someone asked what the fence was like, and I said, 'Natural cedar, with a beautiful greenish hue.' One of the councilmen asked if I would paint the fence, and I said, 'Surely, with my background, *I* should be the judge of that!' So I lost." He laughed. "It was my Irish streak. They said I'd have to take the fence down, but I didn't, and finally City Hall asked me to take it down three or four inches. So we compromised all around."

"Erickson doesn't sound Irish to me," I said.

"My father's family were dour Swedes, but my mother's family, the Chattersons and McKnights, were English and Irish, terribly full of fun and vitality," he said, leaning back in his chair with his hands behind his head.

Hilborn House, Cambridge, Ontario (1974)

"A . . . hillside house . . . had an impossible site in Ontario . . . the clients were extremely conventional and really wanted a little English cottage . . . I told them I had a wonderful place to grow their vegetables and for him to mow his lawn. He asked, 'What's that?' and I said, 'The roof.'—because there wasn't much property that could provide lawn space. Now he is very proud of his vegetable garden."
—Erickson

Graham House, Vancouver (1963)

"My clients have never been normal clients; they have always had impossible sites. They would apologize to their friends and say, 'Well, really we had to get Erickson because the site was so impossible.'"
—Erickson

"My mother, who died in 1979 at the age of eighty-four, inherited my Irish grandmothers extraordinary zest for life, along with my English grandfather's originality and argumentativeness. *His* father was an Ontario teacher and amateur doctor who wrote a book about herbal medicine. My grandfather was a big, fat man and a sort of black sheep—he could never settle into anything. He was a policeman, then a private detective, but first he was a wheat farmer in Brandon, Manitoba, near Winnipeg. That's where my mother was born."

When the farm buildings were blown away in a tornado, the Chattersons moved to Winnipeg, and after their daughter married Oscar Erickson they followed the young couple to Vancouver. The Chattersons opened a chocolate-and-ice-cream store there. "It was famous for the best chocolates in Vancouver, called Mary Jane's," Erickson continued. "Since my grandmother insisted on pure cream and the best eggs and chocolate, they could never make any money, but the place was delightful for us children. We loved to dip the molds for chocolate Easter bunnies. My grandparents came every Sunday for dinner and my grandfather, a radical, argued about *everything* with my father, who was a conservative. My grandmother used to take my brother and me on marvellous walks for four or five hours—always to collect something: pebbles, mushrooms, moss, leaves, flowers. In Manitoba they had traded with Indians, and she told us that if she had had her choice she would have been an Indian or a gypsy, because Indians and gypsies had freedom and a closeness to

Point Grey townhouses, Vancouver (1965)

Point Grey townhouses, floorplan.

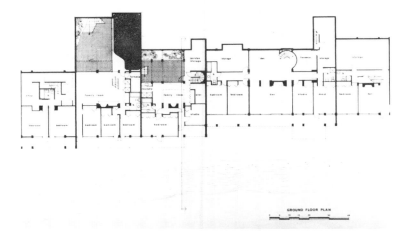

GROUND FLOOR PLAN

nature. The whole walk was always a discovery, and since she was an avid reader, who read a book a night, she would fascinate us while we walked with a story made up from all six books she'd read that week. We would be entranced, in suspense all the time.''

His father, Oscar Erickson, lost both legs in the First World War. A shell burst between his knees at the battle of Amiens, blowing one leg off and injuring the other so severely that it was amputated the next day. He had been left for dead on the battlefield but was recognized by an acquaintance who was a nurse there and taken to a field hospital. Before going overseas in the Seventy-eighth Winnipeg Grenadiers he had been engaged to Myrtle Chatterson in Winnipeg, where he was employed as the western sales manager with E.H. Walsh & Company, a drygoods firm. A handsome, somewhat haughty young man, he grew up in Toronto, and prior to the war had been a fine athlete, excelling at track. After his injury everyone, including Captain Oscar Erickson, thought that the wedding would be off—everyone but Myrtle Chatterson. ''It was an awful thing to have happen to anyone, especially someone who loved sports,'' she remarked shortly before her death. ''But I said, 'I'd rather marry a man with wooden legs than a wooden head.' I worried before I saw him again about how I would feel, but I never changed. He had a terrible time learning to walk, but he never complained. I think it made both the boys more serious—especially Arthur.''

When Oscar Erickson returned to Winnipeg, he persuaded his former

Oscar Erickson.

''I got my painting interest from my father. He had a good water colour technique, but I would not say his painting was good, although he was doing it all the time. He made our Christmas cards every year. I always wrote a poem for special events— Christmas, Easter, birthdays.''
—Erickson

Arthur (left) with Donald Erickson and grandmother.

''My grandmother— my mother's mother—was a marvellous woman who could sing and dance and play piano by ear. She had enormous energy and in her sixties climbed a mountain without running out of breath at all. All my friends adored her.''
—Erickson

Myrtle Erickson, with her two sons, Arthur (left) and Donald.

"Did I have a happy childhood? Yes and no. Yes, because something was always happening. My mother was a great entertainer and there were always interesting people about. No, because I was shy and sent to play with people I didn't like. I much preferred being with adults."
—Erickson

Fish paintings on bedroom wall.

"I thought I would like to paint fish on my walls, which my father thought foolish. My mother said, 'Paint them and then take him up to look at them', so she stole his paints and gave them to me and said, 'Paint while he's away.' I did, two very small fish on a pale green wall at first, and then I did a Rousseau type jungle for my brother."
—Erickson

firm, who thought amputees should retire on pension, to take him on as a commission agent and to let him open new territory outside of Vancouver. After he was fitted with artificial legs he learned to walk with canes, and he once climbed a mountain sideways to look at a gold mine he was interested in. He learned to drive a hand-operated car, and he worked as a manufacturer's agent until he died in 1965. He liked to entertain his children with stories about the war, and he kept up his interest in athletics. "He was so disappointed that neither of the boys liked sports," Mrs. Erickson recalled. "The first race Arthur ran, he said to me, 'Oh, Mother, I don't want to run,' and when my husbance put both boys in the Seaforth Cadets, a boys' training corps for the army, Arthur said, 'I just can't click my heels fast enough!'

All his life Oscar Erickson visited hospitals to encourage other double amputees, served on the Vancouver Parole Board, and pursued his favourite avocation—painting from nature, chiefly flowers. The Ericksons never lost touch with the nurse who saved Oscar Erickson's life, Elizabeth Pearce. She was a lot older than they were, and after she retired from nursing in Victoria and moved to Vancouver they had her for dinner every Sunday night, the rest of the family enduring while she and Mr. Erickson refought the war. "Any time we had anything, we asked Elizabeth; we felt we owed it to her," Mrs. Erickson said. In her later life Mrs. Erickson, a slender, brown-eyed, dreamy octogenarian, lived in comfortable disarray in a small apartment ten minutes from both her sons, surrounded by paintings—her own work, done in a delicate Japanese brush style; her husband's traditional flowers; dramatic pastels of a calla lily and a forest scene by Arthur; and a landscape by Emily Carr, which she had on loan for life from Arthur, who bought it before Carr became famous.

"We were brought up as if my father were absolutely normal," Erickson told me. He got up and put a Beethoven string quartet on a record-player in the living room, talking as he moved about. "My mother treated him like anyone else, except that when they built their house in 1919 she insisted, over the contractor's objections, that the main floor be at ground level and that the garage be attached to the kitchen, although such things were not done at that time. My father was very kind and warm, a humble man, but he was very proud too, and until he died he did everything for himself. Stairs were his problem, and if they had no railing and we had to help him he would always apologize. I remember once when I was very naughty as a child, I escaped to the second floor, shouting 'You can't catch me!' because I had never seen my father climb that many stairs. I never saw anyone get up those stairs so fast. I don't know to this day how he did it." With a smile, Erickson continued, "There wasn't one thing my parents agreed upon except that they loved one another. I think that was good. My mother had Socialist leanings, and my father was a Royalist. He had got the Military Cross from King George V. He had sung in an Anglican church choir as a boy and went to Anglican services sometimes as an adult, but we were

brought up Christian Scientists. My mother tried all the denominations after my father was wounded, and found that one the most optimistic. I came back from Sunday school one day when I was six or seven and told my father he could get his legs back, and shortly after that I dropped Christian Science, but a religion so optimistic is a lot better than an attitude of sin and guilt. However, I have suffered ever since from trying to adjust to the presence of evil in the world. Deep inside, I am convinced that everything is basically good."

He was leaning back now, staring up at the skylight, through which the sun was streaming, illuminating the plants. He continued, "Our house was full of young people, and we could do anything we wanted. I've met so many young people who are victims of their parents, but ours gave us their complete confidence, and we inherited that trust and acted on it. They were secure and selfless people, always doing for others, not really concerned about themselves, although my father had a lot of discomfort he could have complained about. In an old-fashioned way, they taught us that our duty was to serve our culture and that that was all we were here for. Although we had no independent income, there was no concern if we had money or we didn't, and that's part of security too. If you feel you must have money, you're insecure if you don't have it. At the same time, every child has to understand that the basic reality is economic survival. When I originally announced my intention to be a painter, my father said, 'How are you going to make a living?' And when I went to the university he said, 'Now you

have to take care of yourself.' During high school I always worked summers in fishing and logging camps."

Mrs. Erickson, an inspired cook, loved to give parties on the spur of the moment—a trait Erickson has inherited—and she involved the whole family in elaborate decorations and culinary preparations. "My father was a very well-organized person, surrounded by disorder, who never knew when or whether he would get his dinner," Erickson continued. "When my mother cooked, there were pots everywhere and sauces on the ceiling. She was equally creative about her wardrobe. She arrived late at the party I gave for her eightieth birthday because she was painting her shoes grey to match her dress. Not long after that, she went to another party and at the last minute painted her shoes green and had to put them in the oven to dry. Her friends had just bought a new white carpet, and the next morning they called and said, 'Myrtle. Did you by any chance paint your shoes again?' 'Yes, I did,' she said. 'Why?' 'Because there are large green tracks across our carpet,' they said."

Mrs. Erickson had more conventional painting interests as well. In the late thirties, when Canadian painters were unrecognized in Canada, she organized

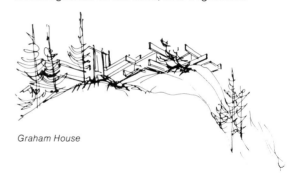

Graham House

an annual exhibition and sale called, "Do You Own a Canadian Painting?" After her husband's death she herself began painting, with a group of women who called themselves the Yellow Door Studio. Erickson occasionally joined them to share a paperbag lunch with his mother, which always contained something unexpected: the last time he went with her, she had picked up the garbage by mistake.

At thirteen Erickson began to paint, making a timid copy on his bedroom wall of two very small fish from photographs in the *National Geographic*; he used his father's paints while his father was away. Having gained confidence and a set of oil paints of his own, Erickson covered all four walls of his room with exotic fish and other fauna. Then he created such an irresistible jungle of plants, birds and animals in his brother's room that Donald brought his friends home for target practice with a BB gun, until the plaster started falling down. Erickson's first professional painting was a stylized horsey hunting scene, done when he was in high school—a mural for the basement of a friend of his mother's, which took him several months and for which he was paid fifty dollars. He then began doing abstract pastels, and two of them received honourable mention in a show at the Vancouver Art Gallery where, at sixteen, he was the youngest artist to have exhibited. Shortly thereafter, Lawren Harris, one of the Group of Seven—the first Canadian artists of stature to break away from the European tradition and paint their own landscape—came, with his wife, to Erickson's house to see his work. "Harris seemed quite indifferent

Erickson at age 17.

"There is another story about Arthur painting things—he was supposed to go to a party wearing a black tie and couldn't get to the cleaners in time to get his shirt so he painted his chest white with oil paints and painted buttons on and a little bow tie, and wore his tux."
—Donald Erickson

Erickson as army radio station operator, World War II.

"In the radio station, I would advertise for talent from the troops. I got a BBC announcer, an Old Vic player, and a news writer, plus local talent. I lived in a marvelous house on a hill, and our only hardship was our K rations."
—Erickson

Opposite: Erickson sketches from early travels.

What the well dressed man will wear!
outside a station near Calcutta

Black Tusk Painting

"I did it in pencil first, sketching with the Botanical Club in Vancouver that summer, and when I got home I developed it as a large composition. This was my most mature painting, a kind of peak, and from then on the intensity of my painting was dissipated and I began to repeat."
—Erickson

Erickson and mother at reception for Order of Canada award, Ottawa (1973)

41

to my paintings," Erickson told me, "but a month later he phoned to borrow my sketch of the Black Tusk, a mountain crag in Garibaldi Park near Vancouver, for an exhibition of American nonobjective painters." The Harrises and the Ericksons became fast friends. The Harrises filled a void in Vancouver cultural life; having come from the East, they had intellectual ideas and an elegant life style that Erickson much admired. "Every Saturday night, the Harrises opened their house and the literati of Vancouver arrived at eight sharp," he said. "You sat for three hours in the dark listening to an extraordinary collection of records on probably the finest hi-fi setup in the city, with very interesting people. I was sixteen, and terribly flattered to be included. A whole different world opened to me."

A high school teacher, Jessie Faunt, gave him his first inkling of design. "She was overjoyed by painting and transmitted this to her students," said Erickson. "I *really* began painting then. I remember being absolutely overwhelmed by a sudden vision of the grand design that pervades nature, the sense of everything's following a certain rhthym. At fourteen, you have very intense feelings, and I felt that this vision gave me the power to capture the truth of *anything*. I would be up until two or three in the morning, sketching. It was kind of a refuge, too. I had a lot of friends, but I didn't enjoy baseball and football, and I was terribly shy. My father thought going to war was your duty to your country and started my very young in the Seaforth Cadets, which I hated. That and the Boy Scouts—I hated it all.

Any regimentation is anathema to me."

Erickson no longer paints, and his drawing is limited to architectural sketches. "My painting ideas were original, but I wasn't very good technically," he said. "I am much more interested now in space and landscape and light. My father suggested architecture as an area in which I could use my creative instincts. I had toyed with becoming a biologist, but I knew nothing about architecture. Everyone was quite willing to suggest different things—everyone but Lawren Harris. He said, 'Look, Arthur, it's your life, not mine. Therefore, it is your decision.' It was by far the best advice I got, and exactly the advice I give whenever anyone asks me what to do."

By 1942 Erickson had spent one year at the University of British Columbia. "I belonged to the Players Club and I worked on the set for an absolutely dreadful play called *George and Mary*," he said. "I managed to get different companies to donate props, and I foolishly borrowed a whole set of sterling silver from a local jewelry store. Nobody would have known the difference if it had been tin on that stage, and it was stolen." He shuddered. "An awful experience. An *awful* experience. I wasn't thanked for my role in *George and Mary*!"

The Second World War was three years old and his father suggested he join the Canadian Army University Corps, because he could be in the army without losing any time and would be getting a technical background. He joined up and undertook an engineering program, but after a year he was invited to enroll in an intensive Japanese

43

University of Lethbridge, Lethbridge, Alberta (1971)

"At Lethbridge . . . we went further than Simon Fraser. The windows had to be reduced, [and] we tried to combine everything in one building, even the residences . . . They could use all the laboratories when they wanted, the library and everything else so that all the University was available all of the time; and why shouldn't it be?"
—Erickson

Lethbridge University

language course. (At least once a year he still goes to see his former teacher, a Japanese woman who lives in Vancouver, and he can speak enough Japanese to get along in Japan.) A year after he began his studies he was in India with a commission, fifty pounds of Japanese dictionaries and no basic training, learning to be a commando in a field broadcasting unit which was to be sent behind enemy lines to demoralize Japanese troops. Luckily, when Erickson's group was on its way to the infiltration point in Malaya, the Japanese surrendered and the group didn't have to go behind the lines. He was then kept in Malaya as a program director for Radio Kuala Lumpur, although he had never been inside a radio station. "We broadcast in nine languages, none of them Japanese," Erickson said, laughing. "Nobody was listening, or cared what we did, so we put on marvellous plays, terrific music, great poetry readings, and every Thursday, our day off, we went tiger hunting. I went along for the walk, the scenery and the plants."

Some months after the end of the war Erickson returned to Vancouver. He was still thinking of becoming a painter, but nevertheless he spent the summer of 1946 brushing up on economics, history and Japanese, with a diplomatic career in mind. "Diplomacy allows you to have painting as a hobby, so my father agreed to that," he said. "I enjoyed the history, except that I never believed what teachers taught—that history was a series of events such as wars and coronations, or that history is affected by human decision. I believe history has to do with the development of a culture,

and that the individuals involved are only agents of the evolutionary process."

It was noon, and Erickson went to the stove to fix us some lunch. "I am utterly grateful that I didn't go into diplomacy," he said, putting a pan on the stove, breaking eggs into a bowl, and stirring furiously while he talked. "I have fairly good manners, but I could never have taken orders to act in a way I didn't believe in. So I was thinking about anthropology or archeology. Then a friend of my mother's brought over a copy of *Fortune*, containing the first colour photographs of Frank Lloyd

Wright's desert house, Taliesin West. When I saw those pictures I said immediately, 'If you can do as imaginative and creative a thing as that in architecture, I want to be an architect.' I wired all the Eastern universities I could think of—Harvard, Yale, M.I.T., the University of Toronto, McGill. Being a Westerner, I wanted to understand the Eastern mind. It was barely a month before school started, and McGill was the only university I heard from. So I packed my bags and left for Montreal."

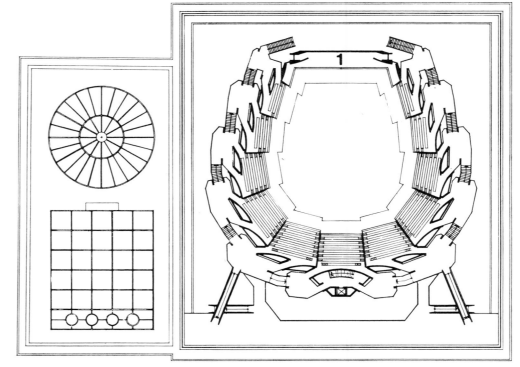

New Massey Hall

Erickson set two heated plates holding omelettes filled with tuna fish and black caviar on the table. "This is called an *omelette en faveur du curé*, and the trick is to turn it out onto a hot dish that has melted butter, lemon, parsley, and chives in it," he said. Back at the counter, he stirred oil and vinegar briskly into a bowl of salad greens, set it down between us, and resumed his seat. "This is special for this Sunday. Ordinarily, my lunch is tea and a sardine sandwich on black bread, with grapes. It used to be sashimi, a Japanese dish of raw fish, when I could get it. I have it at my desk." The music stopped, and he went into the living room and changed records, holding them carefully by their edges. He had started the coffee machine again, and it provided a hissing counterpoint to the melancholy, haunting melody that drifted into the kitchen. "I have music when I work—Bach preferably."

He sat down and began eating. "My whole life in architecture has been a continual unfolding. I enjoyed every minute of my four years at McGill," Erickson said. He and a close friend, Douglas Shadbolt, who is now Director of the School of Architecture at the University of British Columbia, went east to McGill together. "Being Westerners, I think we had a certain brashness, but also a freshness and originality," Erickson continued. "The Eastern mind seemed very conventional. I still find more in common with architects on the West Coast of the United States than I do with those in Eastern Canada. With a Western background, you don't look to any older culture for standards, so unique solutions are the rule. We really appreciated how free we were, coming from the West."

When he finished eating, he sat gazing out at the garden. "I love that river grass out there. Look at the beautiful pattern. And within the pattern are all the variations of Beethoven compressed into a single image."

He picked up the dirty dishes and put them in the sink. "I didn't listen to my teachers much, but I had three people who influenced me—all keenly observant, original spirits," he said, returning to the table. "My mother was the strongest, then Lawren Harris, and I had a design professor at McGill, a painter, Gordon Webber, who has since died. He was a cripple, four feet tall with only one leg and an extraordinary way of seeing. He made you study the potential of materials, following Bauhaus methods. One exercise was to work with every way of folding and erasing paper, and another was to explore the depth of space on paper with floating dots and straight lines. He was original with photography, too. We had to photograph the effect of light on paper and on solid forms, and do our own darkroom work. He was very vague, never explained anything clearly, which forced you to see for yourself. I don't think I would be as receptive to everything as I am had it not been for Gordon Webber."

The summer before his final year at McGill, Erickson went to see Frank Lloyd Wright at Taliesin East in Wisconsin. "The taxi dropped me at the bottom of the hill the house was built on," Erickson said. "I walked into a sort of stable filled with at least a dozen cars and trucks—among them, two Lincoln Continentals—all painted Wright's favourite colour, Cherokee red. I emerged into a beautiful courtyard of

Canadian pavilion, Osaka World Fair (1970)

"I lived, ate and slept Osaka for months. We were shooting for an invisible something, original and out of character for world fairs. How do you make a garden for everyone to relax in, an invisible building, and then make it representative of Canada? We were all working on it but Arthur had the insight into the appropriate symbols. He let in drama with his mirror walls reflecting sea and sky. It was an incredible combination of nothing and something: magic. No other way to describe it."
—Bruno Freschi

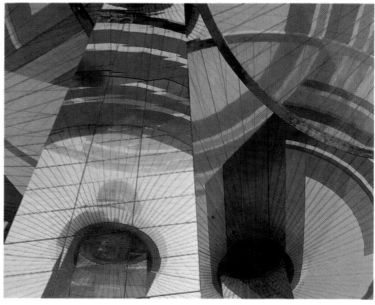

Top: main entrance. Bottom: rotating umbrellas. Opposite: reflecting walls.

48

somehow rescued," he told me. "The idea of peace and retreat was terribly attractive, but I believe now that you have to be in the thick of things. It might have taken years and years to recover."

Erickson's travelling scholarship gave him fifteen hundred dollars, and he managed to stretch that, an eight-hundred-dollar veteran's grant and free passage he wangled on a freighter taking dynamite to India in July, 1950, into almost three years of travel through the Middle East, Europe, and Scandinavia. Originally he had planned to get off in England and attend the Festival of Britain, but at the last minute the boat he was on changed its route, and he disembarked in Egypt instead. He spent a quarter of his funds in the first ten days of his journey, at a reunion with old friends in Cairo, and with eighteen hundred dollars left, vowed never to look anybody up again. He travelled third class from then on, and when he needed socks he had them sent from home—preferably grey ones, and only two pairs at a time, he explained. "No more, because they become a responsibility," he wrote.

"When I started in Egypt, I had no interest whatsoever in historical architecture," Erickson said. "McGill had just thrown off the yoke of traditional, beaux-arts training, so I had been taught with a very disparaging look at the past. In Egypt, with its revelations of extraordinary beauty and vitality of the past, I lost my interest in the new immediately, and became absorbed in the sequence of architectural development. I decided then to travel historically, to follow the whole development of western architecture."

He departed from Cairo to Beirut, booked as a deck passenger on an elegant Italian liner, spending his first night out sleeping under a lifeboat on the first class deck. "I looked down the next morning on a seething mass of miserable people crammed into the prow on the second deck below," Erickson went on. "I asked the well-dressed passenger standing next to me who they were, and he said, 'Oh, they are the deck passengers.' Then, in Lebanon, I started on my pilgrimage in third class buses, living in the worst accommodations, whatever was cheapest."

Everywhere he went he photographed the indigenous architecture, mailing home the undeveloped film; his collection of pictures taken on his travels—he does not photograph his own work—has now proliferated into fifteen thousand colour slides. They are always two-and-a-quarter inches square to give a wide-screen effect when reproduced, are almost all taken in clear sunlight and largely unpeopled; his eyes are focussed on spaces and buildings. Jack Shadbolt, the artist, a brother of Douglas Shadbolt, once observed, "That way you concentrate on the aesthetics of the slides, which is Arthur's temperament."

Erickson has graduated from an early Rolliflex to what he proudly describes as "the same kind of Hasselblad camera the astronauts employed to photograph the earth." Francisco Kripacz, his frequent travelling companion, owns the camera and does not permit Erickson to carry it. "If it was his own, it would be a total wreck," Kripacz has remarked. "Anything with machines, he bangs around. Before he rented cars he never changed the oil on his own, and often landed in the middle of the street without gas. Now he doesn't stay long enough any place to use up a tank of gas, which the rental agency fortunately provides."

On that first trip, Erickson kept up a steady flow of critical comment homeward. Spain, with its siestas and late dinners, he pronounced not conducive to work. "The death of a country rests . . . on the hour of its meals"; Tangiers was "a perfect place to rot . . . a refuge for Europeans who have escaped from Europe for an aimless indulgent life . . ."; postwar England, "a tragedy that belittles Hamlet, shames Oedipus, dwarfs . . . the collapse of Rome . . . . An empire, a

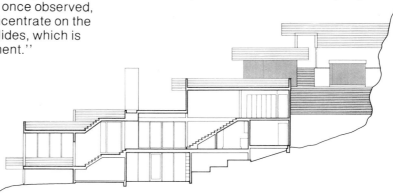

Graham House

51

King Faisal Air Force Academy, Al K harj, Saudi Arabia (1980)

"A military academy proposed to have the cadet houses arranged around the academic core in order to achieve as compact a building complex as possible because walking in this climate is pretty difficult. It was an attempt to reach a design that fitted the desert landscape. The water towers provide a canopy for the whole project."
—Erickson

Top: Model photograph overall. Bottom: Model of mosque, interior. Opposite: Academy mosque.

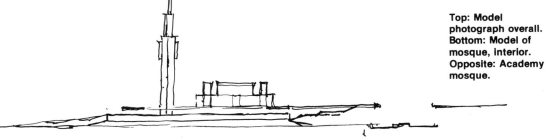

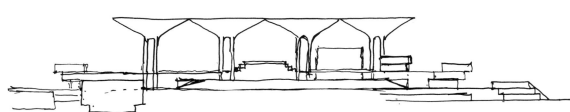

52

Erickson travel photo of receding doorways, Angkor Wat, Cambodia

Lethbridge University, perspective of doorways.

extraordinary peace and quiet, where the only sound was a swish from a branch of pine as a jet of water from a pool hit it and pushed it out of the way and it came back. I walked up the hill to the top, where you could look over the house, which was built around but not on the summit, and see the whole countryside—an absolutely beautiful blending of building and landscape. When I entered the foyer of the house someone was playing a harpsichord, and I felt that this was what a medieval monastery must have been like. At my interview Wright was completely charming, with a Welsh twinkle, and immensely flattering, because he seemed interested only in your opinions, your future, what you believed in, what your background was. It was a Sunday, and later everyone assembled in their best clothes in the living room, and then Wright and Mrs. Wright came in and sat on special chairs, with everybody at their feet. I remember my feeling of dismay at all the false ceremony. I felt that this was really Mrs. Wright, and that Wright went along with it, with a nice little sense of humour, because he enjoyed being starred.''

Wright invited Erickson to Taliesin for the year, offering to let him pay the eleven-hundred-dollar tuition whenever he could. Erickson, jubilant, returned to McGill to pack his belongings. But when he informed the director of the School of Architecture, John Bland, of his plans, he found that he was in line for the next year's travelling scholarship, awarded annually to the best graduating student; he stayed. ''Sometimes there is a door you could have gone through that would have changed your life, and you are

50

whole intrinsic stage in the stair of civilization . . . breaks up helplessly with the muffled thunder of spring ice.'' He also sent his parents a new design for their garden. ''My plan is a simple one, but expensive,'' he wrote on the rough sketch, which included a scheme of elaborate plantings and a pool ''to reflect the distant mountains.''

Italy suited him best, and he stayed there longest. He wrote home to his parents that he ''never knew that so much bad painting had been done'' until he visited the museums in Venice, and that the interior of St. Mark's was distinguished for its ''ineptitude,'' but that Venice was ''not far from those projected ideal cities in management of traffic, for the pedestrian walks unimpeded by any vehicle.'' He was entranced with Florence. ''Collected in this small space,'' he wrote, ''is most of what has given us the reason and desire to reach this present moment in history . . . the impetus to send us staggering to now.''

Florence held him for nine months. An organized daily regime of sightseeing took him inch by inch through Florence and into the environs, where he visited that ancient high priest of art, Bernard Berenson, at his villa, I Tatti. ''He gave me names of marvellous places I would never have gone to otherwise,'' Erickson said now, leaning back again with his hands behind his head and gazing up at his skylight-greenhouse. ''I lived in a bathroom in Florence, using a mattress on top of the bathtub. There was a tavern in a basement on the Via Cavour, where all the students in Florence seemed to eat, and there I met an artist, Carl Massa, who was a

passionate worshipper of Michaelangelo, and used to take me for days just to look at his work and explain it to me. He scorned the early David and the early *pietas* as concessions to Florentine taste at the time, with their concern for detail—all the veins in the arms, the curls, and the folds in garments. He showed me how in Michaelangelo's later works, ''the surfaces become rougher, the detail more obscure, until in the last *pietas* and other sculptures the figures barely emerge from the stone; only to show what's necessary to convey the intensity of the meaning. No concession to the taste of the time in them! I feel that something happened then that affects me whenever I am looking over my own work. Anyhow after nine months I was still rushing around trying to cram in a few things I hadn't yet been able to see. Vancouver is my home, but I have always thought of myself as a Florentine, although now I would like to live in the maturity of Rome.'' He suddenly shifted position, bringing his elbows down on the table in front of him and resting his chin in his hands. ''That trip was the best thing that ever happened to me,'' he said. ''I was

thrilled by the originality and audacity of the early builders. The commanding presence of buildings that exuded an inner life became the criterion of great art for me. I believe we live our lives backward anyway—that everything is known and that somehow we have to go through it once again. As a North American, I had always looked for roots. I discovered that our culture, thoughts, sense of form and space were very much part of the Western experience from the twelfth century on. Part of anyone's quest is to find the missing pieces in whatever mosaic it is necessary for him to function in, and I needed to know''—he paused—''why I am what I am.''

In London, at the end of the trip, he took a job assisting the architect son of Sigmund Freud, Ernst. ''He wasn't a very good architect, but it was a fascinating experience,'' Erickson said. ''I worked for him on a competition project, and his office was in his garage. Every afternoon we came into the house for tea, and there were always amusing people there. He paid me twelve pounds a week, which was about thirty-five dollars then, and it was awfully difficult to live on.''

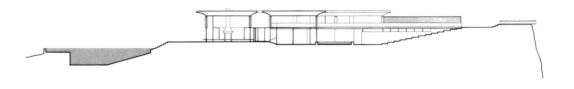

Filberg House

54

On his return from Europe, Erickson worked for several major Vancouver architectural firms and got fired from two. "I would have fired me today," he said. "I was looking at things too differently. One firm was designing the main Vancouver post office and I suggested using different layers of glass to make its enormous mass less heavy and give the illusion of depth. Highly impractical and costly. I wouldn't do that now. Really, I was a dreamer and not much use. I wasted a lot of their money. At that time I also was host on a televison program with local artists. It only ran for eight programs, an hour each, and it was hysterical, it was so bad. I had a potter on one show, one of those creepy uncommunicative types the way potters often are, and I didn't know much about pottery, but he knew absolutely nothing." He laughed, got up and stretched, and poured fresh coffee into our mugs.

On the side, Erickson and Geoffrey Massey, whom he met in Vancouver, had begun designing houses for their friends: an earlier dwelling for the Smiths, which won a medal for small-house design; a studio-residence for an artist, Ruth Killam, whom Massey married shortly afterward. Then Erickson began a dramatic pavilion-like structure, with Persian overtones, viewing the magnificent Comox Glacier on Vancouver Island, for Rob Filberg, a wealthy young man whose vision was to establish a cultural centre where world leaders could meet informally and talk. Filberg was having severe emotional problems, and planning the centre seemed to give him a fresh purpose. "I had a feeling that I was in a race against

Filberg House, Comox, B.C. (1958)

"If I could do the Filberg house right now with the same sense of space, it might be a better design. It was in my Florentine period, and rather fancy: concerned with detail and the rarity of each material, whereas now I want to build in one material for the sake of clarity."
—Erickson

Filberg House, Comox, B.C. (1958)

"The design was really based on a pavilion for looking at the landscape, where all the aspects—the cliff edge, the distant glaciers, the sweeping brown fields and the immediate forest, could be seen at once."
—Erickson

Filberg's destruction, and that if he could get into his house with the grand scheme working, he would have the motivation he needed," Erickson said. Filberg died in a freak accident before the house was done. His family commissioned Erickson to finish it as a private dwelling, and it was sold. Erickson can still describe every detail of that landscape—the conformation of trees, fields, orchards, cliffs, and "the ethereal beauty" of the view. "I am an idiot in anything but the visual realm," he said. "I have difficulty remembering such things as names and appointments, but I can walk over any setting in my mind. I never forget one."

Once he has landscaped a site, he is apt to regard basic changes made without his approval as offensive. The landscape around a Vancouver residence he designed was remodelled by a subsequent owner with what he regarded as "extraordinarily vulgar taste." Erickson said, "The property had gorgeous maples with moss, and the new owner started by taking down the maples and filling the space in with tennis courts and guest houses. It doesn't annoy me, it infuriates me! She keeps saying, 'You must come over and see what I've done'—but over my dead body, I'd go!"

Erickson began teaching architecture in 1955, at the University of Oregon. The following year he joined the faculty of the University of British Columbia, which had turned him down when he first came back from Europe. He taught there until 1964, leaving a year after he and Geoffrey Massey jointly won the competition for the design of Simon Fraser University and formed a

57

Erickson travel photo of teahouse, Saihoji temple, Japan

Erickson travel photo of Kokedera Temple garden, Japan

"In Japan, man doesn't enter into the composition except as an observer. Instead, it is nature that is built around, which infuses the design. The most articulate and reverent space is not the shelter but the garden."
—Erickson

**Opposite:
Eppich House,
Vancouver, (1974)**

Katsura Palace, Japan

"Katsura climaxed all previous experiences. It is the most complete work of art in Japan and I think in the whole repertory of architecture, one of the greatest compositions. More than any other building in Japan, it demonstrates the sense of refinement, of restraint, of severity, of melancholy, of simplicity that the Japanese can achieve."
—Erickson

Faculty Club, University of British Columbia (1968)

partnership that lasted eight years. In 1973, standing in the mall at Simon Fraser and speaking from a portable lectern that he and Massey had presented as a gift to the university, he told graduating students and guests, "North American civilization is one of the ugliest to have emerged in human history, and it has engulfed the world. Asphalt and exhaust fumes clog the villages . . . Holiday Inns proliferate in Afghanistan, Nepal, and Bali; Wimpy Burgers on the Champs-Elysees. This great, though disastrous, culture can only change as we begin to stand off and see . . . the inveterate materialism which has become the model for cultures around the globe . . . Our cities are alive with fake building styles, our homes with fake antiques, our hotels and restaurants and shopping centres with the false pastiche of other lands . . . Disneyland is rife across the land . . . the profound charade that disguises momentarily the emptiness of our souls."

At McGill convocation ceremonies in 1975, he advised graduating students that the "cultural laundering" they had received might make them think they had a "universal expertise" to offer.

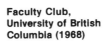

Filberg House

58

"Expertise it may be, universal it is not," he said. "You have been thoroughly versed only in the conceits of your own culture and your own time . . . But to further persist in our view of progress on this earth against all other views is to risk eliminating what little remains of the other great world cultures." Before they could learn, they must "unlearn" and challenge "the old icons of individualism, of progress, of science," so that "other forms may become open to our view."

Rubbing his head, Erickson commented now, "What I said is, 'Forget what all these gurus have told you. It's been a valuable experience. Now forget it. They have been training you in your own cult, and there are many other cults in the world you have to learn.' The students listened in a kind of rapt silence, but I don't think the faculty liked it much. Not one faculty member even *talked* to me afterward."

Former students of Erickson's at U.B.C. remember him as a profound teacher. One of them, Bruno Freschi, describes Erickson's teaching method as "a Socratic, sort of open-ended Zen approach," and explained, "His objective was to turn the person on. Modern architecture is immersed in detail and restrictive therapeutic approaches, whereas Arthur is concerned with design that reflects what he calls timeless dimensions of human behavior. He has a humanist's perception of space, introduces metaphors and symbols into buildings and tries to define the rhthym of human patterns." Freschi continued, "One of the most poetic problems he created was called 'Seven Stones.' He said to the class one day, 'The assignment is to choose seven stones, and present your project in three weeks.' It was terribly generative. Some students danced with seven stones, some glued them to a piece of cardboard, and one got seven beautiful stones from the beach and presented them in a velvet box, clanking them together for everyone to hear. It was a little performance. Arthur looked and said, 'Why are you wearing a blue sweater?' The kid was dumbfounded and replied, 'That had nothing to do with the problem!' And Arthur said, 'No. It's a performance, and your clothing is part of it.'"

I asked Erickson about all this. "I liked teaching, but I could never carry on a career and teach too," he said. "Teaching takes everything out of you. I always made a point of teaching the first-year students, to try and break down the hypocrisy of high school and North American middle-class upbringing." He paused. "I wonder what it is about the middle-class I hate so much? Conventions, I think. Everything is done for reasons other than intrinsic worth. In a creative field, one has to battle this.

"As far as I am concerned, the Socratic is the *only* method of teaching. All my exercises were to force the students to probe their own resources for the meaning of things and not do anything by habit or convention. None of us knew what the problem was, and the whole exercise was to find out. The assignment just to 'choose seven stones' puts students in a state of confusion—a state where there are no answers, only questions. Whenever they come up with what seems like a solution, you take it away, so they have to search deeper and deeper for reasons for their behavior. The choice of the number seven was purely numerical. With *seven* stones, you immediately have questions of grouping, shape, mass, size, colour and texture, and whether to subgroup within the seven. Students climbed to the top of mountains and dived to the bottom of the sea to collect stones. I got in geologists and mineralogists so that we could understand the context of stones as essential ingredients of the earth— which gave them still a different meaning. Suddenly, the stoniness of stone became a fascinating exercise in the history of the earth and of this region. The possibilities were endless, and the students began to realize that with seven stones one could convey practically anything."

Erickson got up and stood with his back against the sink, looking into the garden, as he went on, "During their first year, when I was trying to get them to explore all aspects of their sensitivity, I would arrange a carefully designed dinner, usually Chinese, and then set a problem of designing an unconventional feast, for which they would have to consider light, enclosure, and ambience. I also let a dancer take over the class, to make them aware of their bodies in space, to show how they could explore anything in architecture by movement. One exercise was to draw themselves in a position of movement and then provide a device to support that position out of plastic, wood, paper, or metal. At the end, I pointed out that they had been designing furniture. If I had said, 'Look, we're going to design a chair or a bed,' they would have explored design on the basis of previous memories of chairs or beds. By approaching the model from the opposite, and essential, direction, I was able to make them realize the vital aspects of furniture.''

He sat down. ''Now, how does all this lead to building? I was trying to set up a discipline of approach, so that the students would give any problem the same questioning. This is my own approach to an architectural problem. The method doesn't work on many people. All you can hope to do in teaching is to touch one person—perhaps two—in a class, who begins to realize the force of the elements he is dealing with. Architects are so rarely aware of their own powers of communication, and therefore most of what we see is indifferent building, which nevertheless affects us by its indifference.''

In 1961 Erickson received a federal government grant to study in Japan, Cambodia, and Indonesia, and he had a revelation in Japan which was similar in its impact to his vision at fourteen of the grand design of nature. He had made his usual careful study beforehand of what he wanted to see, and his first stop was Jikko-in, a classical fourteenth-century Zen temple outside the city of Nara, where he lived for ten days. ''I arrived in late afternoon, when nobody was there, and sat on a platform overlooking the garden. It was called a view-borrowing garden, because the hedges were clipped like hills and seemed to extend right out to the hills of Nara. The foreground was raked sand, representing the sea, which gave the

temple the illusion of floating.''

From there, he went to the great Daisen-in temple garden, in Kyoto. ''I was in complete isolation; it was a unique opportunity to experience Japanese life and architecture over a period of five centuries. Unlike us, the Japanese do not move from era to era historically—they pile one on top of another so that an era is never finished but remains alive and vital. Most Western books about Japanese architecture are conditioned by the Bauhaus way of seeing things—especially Mondrian and simple divisions of space. You have to be careful lest your culture screen your vision so that all you see is what you know.'' Erickson helped the priest at Daisen-in write an English guidebook (which was still in use when he returned eight years later), but after three weeks on the vegetarian temple diet Erickson had such an overwhelming craving for sweets and meat that he departed.

Erickson's next stop was the Kokedera, another great temple garden, with two teahouses, near Kyoto—and there he had his revelation. ''I realized that Japanese architecture has nothing in common with Western—it is not designed around the human being,'' he told me. ''It makes no difference where you enter or sit or do anything, because a Japanese building is basically an expansion from the innermost space—to which one retreats in cold weather—outward, right into nature itself.

''One teahouse in the temple garden was a small structure, and all the supporting posts came down on different bases at different heights. One was buried in the ground, another stood on a log beam, and a third on a rock. I was so annoyed at the designer for having decided, without apparent reason, to make each post different that I vowed to stay there, without food or drink, until I solved the mystery. I was there all morning, wandering through

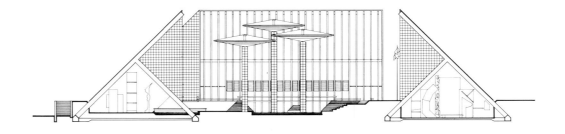

Canadian Pavilion, Osaka

the garden, which was covered with moss and looked as if nothing had ever been pruned or touched but had been allowed to grow naturally. Just as I was asking myself 'Shall I break my vow?' I heard a rustling in the distance, like a flock of birds coming in my direction. From the forest emerged about a dozen men and women gardeners dressed in blue, with baskets for gathering leaves. They put up ladders, climbed them, and then they began pruning the trees. I am accustomed to tree pruning with saws and shears, but these gardeners had scissors the size of nail scissors, and they were giving the pine trees a kind of haircut, removing dead needles, trimming each cluster of needles in their hands, and they were picking the dead leaves off the maples one at a time. The trees seemed to breathe with an openness they hadn't had before, and I realized that here was the secret: I had been looking for what exists in Western architecture—the vitality and strong presence that belong to the human figure, with which we are preoccupied—whereas the whole basis of Japanese perception is nature, the plant, that exists in this extraordinary grace, branching out toward the infinite. If we studied all our lives, we would never have that innate sense of how a tree grows, or wants to grow. I was able to go back to the teahouse then and see that the architect was trying to imply within

Erickson travel photo of Daisen-In Temple garden, Japan.

"The plan of Daisen-in, like all the Japanese Zen temples, had a sort of main compound, with a main gate and main temple. Around it was a walled area in which there were all kinds of gates, and through each of these gates there was a different garden with a different temple of Zen. I was shocked when I went back there just a few years ago to find it had turned into a terrible tourist trap, with souvenir counters. So many people were there they couldn't all get in, and when I was there I lived in complete isolation."
—Erickson

that static structure the same reaching out and upward that occurs in the tree form, starting with a spiralling from one level to another at the very base of the building. I thought, if one needs that kind of revelation to even begin to understand the Japanese, there are still the cultures of the Middle East, Africa, India, and China, which I know nothing about. So I became a dedicated traveller.''

The sun had gone down, and darkness was moving across the green garden. Erickson sprang up. ''Look at that raccoon!'' he cried. ''Bastard! He's fishing at the pool!'' When Erickson opened the door, the raccoon scampered off.

''These observations are not reflected consciously in my buildings when I am designing, because that would be bound to fail,'' Erickson continued. ''But I am sure they find expression superconsciously. I leave everything to the last minute, and it somehow comes together. You get hunches that you have to do something, you simply have to, and they are a terribly accurate indicator. You've got to listen to them. If you don't, you invariably do something wrong. Intellectual reasoning is the narrowest reasoning possible, but your superconscious, which is so much better informed than your conscious mind, is the storehouse of all your experience, and you should be drawing on that to solve any problem.'' He looked at his watch, stretched his arms out in a tired gesture, and said, ''Let's talk again. And one of these days, I'd like to take you through the new courthouse and the museum at U.B.C.''

Theme Pavilion Expo 67

Erickson had been back from his trip to the Far East for two years when he and Geoffrey Massey won first prize in the Simon Fraser University competition. They were supposed to submit a design for a typical American campus, with a separate building for each teaching discipline. ''When Gordon Shrum, the first chancellor of Simon Fraser, announced our names as the winners, we almost fell over,'' Geoffrey Massey told me when I saw him and his wife at his home the next evening. He is a tall, dark-haired man who bears a close resemblance to his father, the actor Raymond Massey. ''We had ignored the requirements, because we thought the university should be a tight complex of elements for use, not of disciplines— with offices, laboratories, and lecture halls arranged in juxtaposition to one another conveniently, to save travel time. We thought we might get a pat on the back for having a good scheme, but we didn't have a hope of winning.''

That was in July, 1963, and Gordon Shrum, who was then chairman of the giant British Columbia Hydro and Power Authority, was following Premier W.A.C. Bennett's orders to select a site, hire architects, build a university for six thousand students, and open it by September 1965.

Shrum, a hyperactive octogenarian, later had the assignment of overseeing the construction of another Erickson-designed project—the new Vancouver Civic Centre complex. His main chore there was to keep a tight hold on the purse strings, since Erickson, like most architects, sometimes has an aptitude for overspending.

Shrum recalls the genesis of the university design very precisely: ''The Premier called and said, 'I have this report by the President of the University of British Columbia saying we need another university in the Fraser Valley. I want you to be chancellor, build it, and have it operating in two years.' I was thrilled. I thought, God, he might change his mind, so I said, 'I better say yes, right now.' I flew in a little B.C. Hydro company plane over the Fraser Valley and decided that the imaginative thing was to put the university on top of Burnaby Mountain. I arranged a competition, open only to B.C. architects. I thought, I'll get ideas from all these young men. They had to submit three drawings: a plan, a perspective, and an elevation, which is a facade of the building. Any architect, or a firm, could enter, and the first five winners could take a five-thousand dollar prize or build one part of the university. Three-quarters of the architects in B.C. worked on it, and we eventually had seventy-one entries. There was a seventy-second, but his wife went to the hairdresser on the way to deliver his drawings and missed the deadline.

"*I was completely dizzy, with two hundred and some drawings, but my international panel of judges threw chips like poker chips down on the drawings and whenever a drawing got five chips, they threw it out,*" he continued. "The best joke of the whole thing was that on those seventy-one entries, there was only one set of drawings on which the judges were unanimous—Erickson and Massey's. They had to vote and vote on the others. I wouldn't have selected their drawings as the winner. They were so plain that they would never have caught my inexperienced eye, but the judges took me in and explained what

Simon Fraser University, Burnaby, B.C. (1963). Drawing for architectural competition by Erickson and Massey (first place)

"I worked on the design for Simon Fraser; the mall and the women's residence. Arthur had strong control of the design, and we were trying to follow his guide lines. He's a one-line sketcher, but he's an eloquent delineator. I've learned a great deal from him."
—Bruno Freschi

Drawing for architectural competition, Simon Fraser University. Second place, Rhone and Iredale

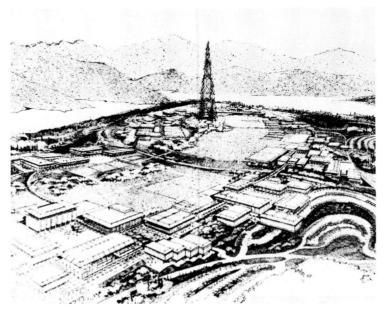

Drawing for architectural competition, Simon Fraser University. Third place, Zoltan Kiss.

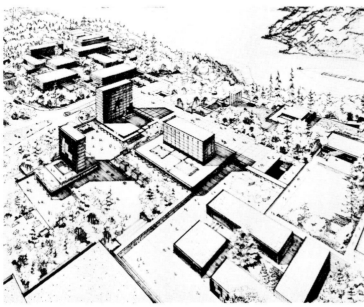

Drawing for architectural competition, Simon Fraser University. Fourth place, R.F. Harrison.

they meant. Arthur's design envisioned one university with buildings linked internally for easy interchange of discipline, not a series of separated affiliated colleges like the University of Toronto, or Oxford. Erickson had built houses and was an associate professor at U.B.C.—not even in business. But if we had chosen anyone else's design, people would never have come from all over the world to see the university, because they could have seen any of the other designs any place. We are mutually indebted to each other. See what he went on to from this!'' He scratched his head, and his eyes gleamed behind his glasses. ''I like to take visitors to Simon Fraser,'' he said. ''You drive along that mountain road and don't see a thing. Suddenly, there it is! Dramatic!''

Each of the four runners-up in the Simon Fraser competition chose to build one of the five original units within the over-all design of the winning architects. Thus, with Erickson and Massey in charge, four essentially rival architecture firms worked on the theatre and gymnasium, the library, the science block, and the quadrangle of offices and classrooms. An Erickson mound crowns the grassy courtyard of the quadrangle —the only detail that makes Shrum nervous. ''I would have preferred a formal garden, like the one at Versailles,'' he says.

The winners chose to build the mall— actually, a three-storey building— because it linked everything together. Erickson has designed several smaller buildings for the university since; the most recent an extention to the mall itself, which will eventually reach the student residential area. He is consulted now whenever construction is anticipated, but during a period of strained relations two structures were put up over Erickson and Massey's opposition—a men's residence, Shell House, which sticks out at right angles to the rest of the design, and a prominent gas station, the funds for both having been provided by the Shell Oil Company.

The original concept of the landscaping was changed as well. "There was to have been a great long lake at the edge of the trees for recreation, and wild grass right up to the buildings," Erickson says. "Poppies grow well in wild grass and reseed themselves, so I thought one way *not* to have the grass cut was to seed it with poppies, which I imported from California. It was summer and we had a poppy planting ceremony at Simon Fraser involving professors, students, all my office and a dancer I got from U.B.C. who came with her own dancers and instruments. We gave each person a square of red cloth, and we had gotten in some cases of wine. None of us had more than one glass but in no time there was this marvellous leaping and waving of red ribbons, with cymbals banging and tambourines, and everybody scattering seed. It was a real pagan rite, ending at sunset, when the dance leader knelt like a high priestess at the head of the steps as the sun came down just on an axis with the quad. Some visitors arrived just then, and I don't know what they thought—maybe that they had come in on some Dionysian rite!" He shook his head, "The grass was cut down anyway. The whole area is criss-

Simon Fraser University

"If Arthur has a weakness, it is that he is a visitor to his buildings and sometimes he designs them as a visitor. The kids at Simon Fraser do get tired of being part of a designed experience, no matter how Zen and open-minded; the only place you get a sense of undesigned space is in the surrounding forest and parking lot."
—fellow architect and teacher

Simon Fraser University. Academic quad.

"Our office did the elevations, the building facades as you would see them from all four sides. We had to design to each other's architecture, and each architect had to build to certain basic elevations, and had to fit a certain height, to plug into a space. The Quad, for instance, had to stay in a square and had to be lifted up to make the view accessible, so it became a building on legs."
—Bing Thom

Simon Fraser University. Classroom block.

"We used the seminar rooms and offices to shape another major space in the centre of the University that would be a quiet and tranquil one. We felt—which was entirely wrong—that students would be social in the social space and tranquil in the tranquil space, but it doesn't work out that way. The main classroom block terraced down the mountain side with flooded roofs. I was romantically recalling the landscape of Bali and its flooded rice fields. What I was also trying to find was a mountain architecture which fitted the slopes and contours of the mountain."
—Erickson

crossed now with roads.''

The students and faculty of Simon Fraser like the place when the sun shines, but rain and fog produce a gaggle of complaints. ''Knocking the university is the 'in' thing to do,'' remarked a student hitchhiker whom I picked up on my first visit there. In wet weather, which prevails twice as often on the mountaintop as in the city of Vancouver just below, the grey concrete has a depressing effect, and the mall becomes a wind tunnel when it's gusty. Everyone grumbles about narrow underground corridors, many of them inserted later by the administration, and small classrooms. ''Magnificent to look at but not to work in,'' says a professor who has been there since the university opened; he feels that the quad offices combine a lack of privacy and a sense of isolation. There have been chronic problems with leaks, and for these the speed with which the concrete was poured has been blamed. Some people complain about the swallows and pigeons that nest under the overhang where the precast cement walls meet the roof. The space-frame roof over the quarter-mile-long mall contained an acre of glass on a wooden truss. Its daring, innovative design by Jeffrey Lindsay, a Los Angleles-based architectural research-and-development specialist, was plagued with construction difficulties. The contractor ordered the wrong glass, and, after an unusually heavy snowfall in 1969, forty-five per cent of the panes broke—1,900 out of a total of 4,224. The mall was boarded over for a few months, and twice as many panes—half the original size—were installed. A complicated series of lawsuits over who was to pay the bill for repairs ensued among the architects, the original roof designer, several insurance companies and the university; the suits were settled out of court in 1975, and Lindsay was paid.

"Our instructions were to build as economically as possible, and that's why we went to concrete," Erickson says. "If the original landscape plan had been followed, the structures would have been covered with vines. When the concrete is wet, it's awfully dark gray, but the better mixes that are available now would still be too expensive. I really *like* concrete. It's the marble of our time—the stone of our century—and it's a natural material of the earth. As for whether the students like the way it is up there, Simon Fraser was a centre of unrest in the sixties, but I knew there wouldn't be serious damage and they would solve their problems, because there was no escaping them. The concentration of people may not be pleasant, but it's important, because it's the reality of life. The basis of culture is the city, and a university should be like a miniature city, to develop an interchange of ideas. What Simon Fraser lacks is a real community, an all-student resident population. Most of the students commute. The university has temporarily abandoned the idea of more residences, but I'm not going to let them abandon it for keeps!"

Erickson has compared his second university, Lethbridge, a long ribbon of concrete which seems to span the valley from one ridge line to another among the Alberta wheat fields, to an enormous ocean liner. Like Simon Fraser, it is a single complex, but its

central focus is an outdoor assembly area on top of a boiler house. "I remembered a Chinese student who designed the furnace of her house in the middle of her living room because, she claimed, it was the heart of the house," Erickson has said. "With the main exterior space of Lethbridge on the boiler plant, its stacks became the symbolic gateway onto the surrounding prairie."

Simon Fraser University. Mall roof.

"Because it rains all the time in Vancouver, we put a glass roof on a wooden truss over the mall. It had to be glass because light is so precious in the North."
—Erickson

Overleaf: Simon Fraser University. Mall from steps of academic quad.

"What Simon Fraser says is that the body of knowledge is one, and that to artificially separate different disciplines and incarcerate them in different buildings completely disallows the kind of cross-fertilization, the chance associations, that have always occurred in our great institutions of knowledge. SFU broke down the university into functional units of work spaces of different sizes and then reassembled them around the students."
—Erickson

IV

Erickson is always ready to try new building materials. He has designed a chrome-plated steel-and-glass residence for the twin brother of the owner of the Eppich House. In 1976, for the visitors' pavilion at the United Nations Habitat Conference in Vancouver, he used recycled newspapers as the basic material for small curved panels, constructed—and decorated with bright, funny paintings—by two thousand schoolchildren. "Five laminations of old newspapers, like an enormous egg crate"—that was Erickson's description of it. "The school children were bussed out to factories, where they laid out their newspapers and glued them into molds. After they had dried, the children came back and decorated them," he said. "We gave the children construction helmets to wear while they were working. They loved it all!"

The Habitat structure's airy charm has reminded Erickson admirers of another experimental cabana beside the swimming pool of a wealthy Vancouverite named Dal Grauer. The material Erickson used then was plastic, and that was before engineers were quite sure how plastic could be used. Like the Habitat pavilion, the Grauer cabana had a lightness, as if it were floating. "He showed his real touch right then," another Vancouver architect commented. "The Grauer cabana was the first time anyone had done anything that frivolous out here. It was so nice!"

The Grauer cabana was one of Erickson's first commissions, and the plastics company that molded the fibreglass forms for him unfortunately went into receivership while three of the panels were still in the plant. "It was hair-raising," Erickson recalls. "I was so anxious not to let Grauer know that the company had gone bust that I had to rent a truck and sneak those panels out at night myself." Erickson's own house has a black shower stall with an oval entrance and a circular flower-shaped cutout in the ceiling which lets in light; the stall is a memento from the same ill-fated plastics company.

Frank Mayrs, the Canadian government's creative director for international exhibitions, a thin man with a wispy mustache and a sympathetic nature, has worked with Erickson off and on since 1965, starting with the first of Erickson's prize-winning international fair structures: a knockdown, prefabricated rough-timber pavilion at the Tokyo Trade Fair which had a pool for logrolling demonstrations. The building that followed for Expo '67, in Montreal, housed the Man in the Community exhibit and has been described by Erickson as "a kind of miniature Eden," with reflecting pools in a tropical garden and an enormous octagonal slatted roof—actually a tent of wood—that decreased in size as it rose to a high opening and seemingly to infinity. Then came the Canadian pavilion at Expo '70, in Osaka, Japan, which was judged the best there by the Architectural Institute of Japan. For both of these pavilions Jeffrey Lindsay was on the design team. The Osaka pavilion was sheathed in mirrors—infinity again—a wall treatment Erickson first saw used in a pleasure pavilion on the end of a lovely garden in Isfahan, Iran. At Osaka, five giant slowly rotating umbrellas in multicoloured designs by Gordon Smith became the roof covering. "The constantly moving mirrored reflections conformed with the Bhuddist concept that nothing is static, but everchanging," Erickson has explained. "It also gave the Japanese, who are earth-oriented, a chance to see all the exciting things that happen in the sky. They called it the 'Sky Pavilion.'"

"You set limits for Erickson, and his proposal is always more than you anticipated," Mayrs told me. "You want to do it, and you immediately run into the problem of cost. He treats his buildings like sculpture and tries to preserve the architectural spaces he creates, even to leaving them empty, when our job demands that the space be booked up, in the traditional exhibit manner. Our pavilion at Osaka was fantastic, but we worried about what effect the reflection of the sun in the mirrors would have on people's eyes, on adjoining buildings, and on the inside temperature. 'You never get direct summer sun in Japan,' Arthur said, but by midsummer the sun was coming straight down, and some buildings around us had to reroute their queue lines. A lot of diplomatic notes went back and forth, and we had to fog the glass with spray paint on one side of the pavilion to check the reflection so we could go on coexisting with our neighbours. When you deal with Arthur, you have to accept heartaches and worries, but the essential thing that must *never* be lost sight of is that the building works."

Mayrs continued, "I knew he would come up with a memorable scheme for Habitat. I got a budget for a hundred thousand dollars, and we talked tents. He did a scheme reminiscent of West Germany's tent at Expo '67, and I O.K.'d it. At the next meeting, there was a totally new scheme—the papier-maché one—which he claimed could be done for still less. It became rapidly clear it wasn't even going to be done for a hundred thousand, and when he said schoolchildren would be involved we finally went up to two hundred and fifty thousand. It was a totally experimental process and the cost, primarily for time, kept escalating, so we had a meeting, and he said he wouldn't cut down, but he did. In terms of a fee, I guess he ended up working for nothing or losing money. It was a wonderful idea to use schoolchildren. It involved the whole city of Vancouver, and that pavilion captured *everyone's* imagination."

Habitat pavilion, Vancouver (1976)

"I wanted a pavilion to demonstrate something to visiting delegates and I got a brain wave: that it should be recycled waste from a basic B.C. product. The first thing I thought of was paper. Our paper shells, six hyperbolic parabaloids made of five laminations of old newspapers reinforced with one of cotton, like cheesecloth, were simple and built by school children. The paper tubing for the edges caused us lots of trouble."
—Erickson

Erickson's addition to the Bank of Canada in Ottawa is a handsome, light, twelve-storey structure of glass and copper, which gives a welcome variety to the grey quality of that city's architecture. The copper was pretreated by workmen imported from Japan for their skill in producing what he felt was just the greenish patina to blend the structure with the surrounding urban landscape of copper-roofed Victorian Gothic Parliament Buildings.

The original plan that Erickson had had for the Bank of Canada had included changes in the entire neighbourhood. Erickson became the Bank's architect after he met Louis Rasminsky, then Governor of the Bank of Canada, at a private dinner party where they had a long conversation about architecture. "He called me one day and said that the Bank of Canada and the Department of Public Works, which had office buildings directly opposite on Sparks Street, wanted to develop the two blocks they were on together," Erickson explained. "The potential was terrific and we proposed a glassed-in mall which would be a kind of winter garden between the two properties. Ottawa's winters are hideously grey and cold and this would have provided green trees the year round, besides reducing the heat loss on the walls on either side of the street, so it made good sense. Sparks Street is one of the busiest thoroughfares in the capital. There is really no place in Ottawa where people can get together except in private clubs. We would have closed one end of the street and we thought, wouldn't it be marvellous to have an area where the public could go for a drink and be able to

Swimming pool cabana, Grauer house, Vancouver (1958)

Canadian pavilion, International Trade Fair, Tokyo (1965)

"Arthur sent a very handsome pavilion to the Tokyo Trade Fair. He sent it over log by log, timber by timber, and he asked Canadian artists to make art for it out of Canadian materials. I did a free-style sculpture out of copper; someone else did one of papier-maché, someone else out of wood, and I remember there was something out of aluminum too."
—Gordon Smith

74

see your Senator at the next table or the Ambassador from Senegal! But the Minister of Public Works, who was Art Laing then, was against it from the beginning. Now there's nothing but a windswept canyon in between, and you can't grow *anything* there.''

Erickson did include a tiny closed atrium on the Bank of Canada's side of Sparks Street, within its own site. The atrium is a small speck of greenery, winter and summer, between the new towers and the old bank building at the entrance of the Numismatic Museum on its first floor, and is visible to passers-by on the street. Twelve storeys high, it contains a large ficus tree, palms and ground plantings, and a pool that Erickson would have stocked with fish if bank officials hadn't thought they would be too much trouble. Erickson regards the atrium as a minor vestige of his larger vision, hardly worth mentioning. ''You get used to disappointments, and I do think the Bank really works with the surrounding landscape,'' he said. ''An awful lot of my buildings are in glass. Funny, I seem to work chiefly in wood and glass and concrete—of modern materials, they are the most natural.''

He brightened. ''Speaking of those materials, I am really pleased with the concrete and glass house I did for the Bagley Wrights in Seattle,'' he went on. ''We spent a long time on that concrete, and it's a beautiful buff colour. The house is a private museum for their painting collection as well as their home, and it's a different demonstration of siting than we've ever done. Usually, we're very careful to save trees, but there I felt a need to cut down a clearing in the forest big enough to get the light

75

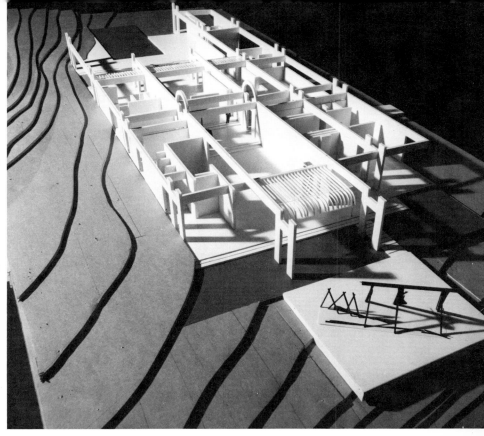

Bagley Wright house, Seattle (1977). Model photograph.

''As always, the landscape was done before the house. The whole piece of property was a forest, and basically, the house follows the idea of a clearing of the forest.''
—Erickson

Second Eppich house, Vancouver (1981). Model photo.

Erickson has ventured for the first time into the use of structural steel for a home, for the twin brother of the owner of the original 'Eppich House.' Most of the furniture and custom-made structural steel for the new house will come from the brothers' own Vancouver factories.

in, and also to see the trees. Virginia Wright's father, Prentice Bloedel, one of the original partners of the MacMillan Bloedel lumber firm, lives on Bainbridge Island in Washington, in a house like a little French chateau, and there he cleared the forest and planted a very tall hedge of yew trees enclosing a formal classical garden with a long pool and lawn. That kind of thing happens in Japan when a temple is built in the forest, and then a wall is built and you see the forest over the wall. But I wanted the forest to act as a wall around the Wright's house. Some of the original trees are a hundred feet high!

"A big concern was also the light coming into the area that would reach the works of art," he continued. "They are in the central rooms, and a glass-block roof diffuses the light to keep the direct sun off the paintings. The house is all wall and paintings, except that it opens to a view of a moving diSuvero sculpture of wood, cable, old logs and chains that is in a meadow at one end, and a huge steel Anthony Caro sculpture set on a platform over the valley at the other end. On one side of the gallery are the Wrights' living quarters and the caretaker's, and on the other side, guest rooms. We used golden-toned stone paving on the floor throughout the house, and very little furniture. Very simple."

Man in the Community pavilion, Montreal World Fair (1967)

". . . Some exhibition architecture . . . is just plain fun. There is nothing serious about it whatsoever, and thank God it is always taken down afterwards . . ."
—Erickson

Glass was to have been the outer covering for a combination high-rise office building and small church to replace the eighty-five-year-old Anglican Christ Church Cathedral, a nondescript structure badly needing repairs, on prime real estate in Vancouver's business district. With a growing deficit, the shrinking congregation decided in 1972 to use its only resource, its valuable corner lot, to put up a revenue-yielding office building into which a new church would be incorporated, and Erickson was chosen as architect. He designed a shaft of steel and glass for the office building, with the church in a separate unit underground, marked above the street by a light-refracting tower rising through a small garden at the corner. Dean T.H. O'Driscoll envisaged the little church as a centre for workshop programs, with the garden "offering a retreat from the street" for passers-by. The congregation approved by an overwhelming vote, and then the heavens fell in on Dean O'Driscoll and his flock.

"I would have said that the difficulty would be within the church and the public won't give a damn," Dean O'Driscoll said. We were talking in his unpretentious study in the shabby nether regions of the cathedral. He was a youngish man in a dark business suit, wearing a rueful expression. "A building eighty-five years old is harder to do away with than if it were eight hundred; people equated their life cycle with this building. They were born and grew up with it, married and buried from it. It became an issue on hot-line shows, in meetings and in every newspaper across Canada, by the time the Vancouver City Council had said 'No, no,' to the building permit. Arthur, who is a mix of architect, poet, philosopher, and mystic, took an attitude of detachment. If anyone could have pulled it off, it would have been Arthur, and it must have been an unpleasant experience for him."

Architectural designs are extremely costly to produce in presentation form for prospective clients, or to enter in competitions for proposed multi-million dollar buildings. Architects may receive some payment to offset their expenses, particularly if a government is involved. In competitions, five or six finalists may receive grants of, say, fifty thousand dollars each to prepare plans. The actual expense of working up a plan can run to double or triple that amount, and normally only one person, or if it is a consortium, one group, wins. All leading architects must deal with this hazard as part of their overhead; all have design projects that were never built.

Christ Church Cathedral is one of a number of Erickson's never-built designs that are still remembered; another commissioned in the early sixties in Montreal is known as M-3. The Canadian Pacific Railroad wanted to develop six acres of land over its railroad tracks in Montreal, and its development firm, Marathon Realty, hired Erickson and Massey, in a joint venture with a Montreal architect, David Boulva, to plan a balanced community with shopping and recreational centres for ten thousand families, approximately thirty thousand people. The partners designed two curved buildings in an enormous spiral to conform to the spaghetti pattern of railroad tracks underneath that were surrounded by freeways and cloverleafs. Meanwhile

Christ Church Cathedral, Vancouver (1973)

"The chancel would have been lit by natural light, coming in through the prism."
—Erickson

"I really wonder about Erickson's hope of lighting the church by prism light going down. I am not sure it would have worked in the ultra greyness of our climate, but he felt it would have been a gentle light, consistent with our coast."
—Dean O'Driscoll

Intelstat Headquarters, Washington, D.C. (1980). Rendering for architectural competition (second place finish).

"The low buildings were arranged in a finger plan—a lot of wings completely covered inside a glass cocoon, which provided an intermediate climatic zone between the inside and outside. No energy was required for heating, and a minimum for cooling."
—Erickson

National Gallery of Canada, Ottawa (1977). Model photograph.

"We had really worked out an ingenious system, and it was a typical public servant reaction to go the wrong way. A normal building has five sides exposed, but by sinking ours into the cliff, only one side was exposed, which would be your opening to the sky for solar heat."
—Erickson

the architects kept suggesting to the developers that the design would be more successful for fewer people. They imported a Boston sociologist to assess the effect the buildings would have on tenants. He predicted a "social disconnection", a detachment from the ground which would come from riding in the elevators. The buildings sloped from a few storeys in shopping areas to forty at the maximum, and he suggested some way be devised for walking up and down, but not on stairs that were enclosed. "You could walk up on the roof of our building or take a series of escalators that were glassed in but exposed to the outside view, going from planted terrace to planted terrace, until you reached your destination," Erickson said. "On good days it would have been marvellous coming down forty floors on all those planted, terraced roofs." M-3 was abandoned because the city of Montreal refused permission for such population density on the six-acre space.

Periodically there is a competition for a new National Gallery of Art in Ottawa. "Most of us have done a design or two for a new Gallery, but there simply doesn't seem to be the money to build one," Erickson says. The latest competition, in 1977, was won by John Parkin of Toronto, with a system of box-like structures strung together whose chief asset is thought to be that they can be constructed gradually. All the designs had to deal with the ninety-foot-high stack of the central steam plant for Parliament Hill, right next to the Gallery site. From the street, the steam plant itself appears to be underground, but is actually on the edge of the cliff with its windows facing the Ottawa River.

"Parkin collected buildings around that stack and created a fortress," Erickson has remarked. "We—David Boulva and I, again in a joint venture—tried to do exactly the opposite. We had the stack as a piece of sculpture right in the middle of the galleries. In our plan, the National Gallery is actually sunken, and we tried to make the whole building act as a terraced cliff side with plantings, by setting the major galleries into the cliff and using their terraced roofs and the power plant roof as extensions of the public plaza to the river. You would have entered from the street side into a vast open space, and our design was arranged so that you could see from the entrance into every gallery and know where to go. Beyond, the view would have been a planted ravine set with sculpture; from that same entrance you looked down under a series of bridges—the four or five storeys of galleries whose terraces were potential areas for works of art—to the wild river and across to the city of Hull, in Quebec. There were big garden spaces, to give you relief from museum fatigue, that you could go out to from the gallery wings. With a collection as large as the National Gallery possesses, you need not only wall space but rest space, or you are overwhelmed."

The design that Erickson regretted putting aside perhaps more than any other was for a badly needed medical centre in Vancouver, planned during the brief, three-year period in the mid nineteen seventies when the New Democratic Party was in power in British Columbia. "When I was approached by the NDP Government, I said I wasn't interested unless they permitted me to be innovative, and

Marathon Realty M-3 Development, Montreal (1968). Plasticene massing model.

"M-3 was a fantastic venture and a beautiful answer to the problem. But it isn't significant to what Arthur is today. More so is the Provincial complex in downtown Vancouver, and the UBC Museum."
—Geoffrey Massey

Opposite: rendering of M-3.

British Columbia Medical Centre, Vancouver (1976)

"Hospitals of ancient Greece gave the patient the best diet, in the best architecture, and contact with the great philosophers and one's religion. The mind and the soul were part of the cure. We of the west have a long way to go to equal that. We might get another chance to do another hospital, and if we do, all that I have learned will be of enormous value."
—Erickson

they replied that the reason they came to me was that they wanted something different and new," Erickson said. "I couldn't resist, but it took a long time to sift through my own mind what a medical centre was meant to be.I had been quite ill several years before with a very bad attack of colitis from nervous tension," Erickson said, and I remembered that the worst thing about it was not the sickness but the demoralization. I also kept remembering one of the most beautiful places I have ever been, on my student travels in Turkey in 1950. In the ancient Greek ruins at Pergamus was a health centre at the head of a valley with a library, a temple to the God of Health, a bath, a theatre and a curative spring and hanging right out over the valley in one corner was the round building for the hospital beds. All the arts were there in their finest form. From the beds and from the colonnade there was a view down the valley for miles. Here was beauty in every aspect; the treatment was of the whole person. By exposure to the finest things, you regained confidence, and faith in your culture and yourself. Before the B.C. Government changed and our scheme was dropped, our medical people worked out one of the most innovative plants in North America.

An unusual Erickson design shelved for lack of funds is a projected twelve-storey federal office building in Vancouver that would be constructed on "legs" seven storeys high. Erickson says, "Nobody wants to look at federal offices or even walk by them, so let's get them out of sight, let's put them up in the air!" He describes the projected huge

Federal Government Office Buildings, Vancouver

"We lifted the government offices above ground to free the ground for public use. Only offices where the public comes in contact—a marketplace for government services—are at ground level. We have done fifteen models, and the design is still evolving. Numbers ten and five are entirely different but looking at every one, you can see the evolution."
—Erickson

Ministry of Public Works and Housing Office, Riyadh, Saudi Arabia (1979)

"It was just a proposal, nothing happened. I was really trying to develop a modern translation of an old technique in Islamic architecture; of bringing light through a very small opening at the top." -
—Erickson

Sawaber Housing Development, Kuwait (1976)

"A series of villas with walls piled one on top of the other, housing one thousand well-to-do families, following the traditional privacy of Arabic family life, with no windows looking from one apartment to another. The underspace provides protection from the sun and is a community area. An example of old traditions in a new interpretation."
—Erickson

Town Centre, Fintas, Kuwait (1979)

"The Kuwait government and private developers are looking at Fintas as an Arab town and at the same time as a North American shopping centre. They would probably have been happy to go for an entirely western design. Our plan follows the old pattern of the souk, for its economic base."
—Erickson

building as "floating" or as a "large protecting umbrella" with the space underneath given over to public recreation, information centres, restaurants and a children's museum, to form a new cultural enclave for the city; its neighbours on three sides are a major theatre, the central post office, and the regional headquarters of the Canadian Broadcasting Corporation.

"Unused designs are never stillborn," Erickson says. "They are always on your conscience, and often you try to resurrect them in something else. Our experience in the Middle East is an example of this. We have been involved there in two urban development plans. First, a housing project called Sawaber, in Kuwait, for one thousand upper middle class villas; and because we didn't think it would go ahead, we made it much clearer for a smaller project in the city of Medina, in Saudi Arabia. In Fintas, Kuwait, we were responsible for designing the centre of a projected town of five hundred thousand people, which we think would provide the most exciting shopping centre in the Middle East."

As often happens, especially in the Middle East, Erickson's Sawaber design was bought and paid for but someone else is putting up quite different buildings. In fact, the development drawings were purchased and put out for tender before his firm had worked out all the details. Singapore contractors were the successful bidders and were put in charge of construction. "The clients commission something, you design it, they pay you, and then someone else gets to do it. There should be a law against that," Erickson complains with uncharacteristic

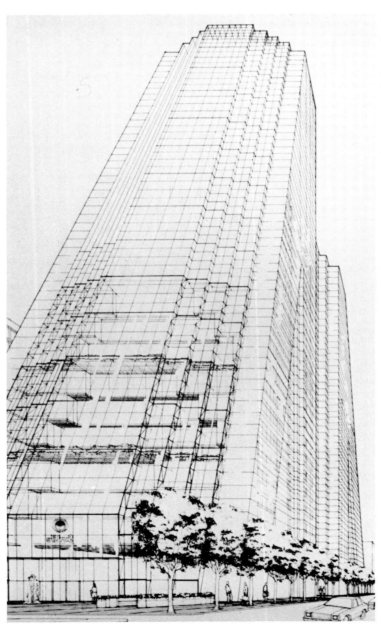

Sun Life Headquarters, Toronto (1980)

"It was a passive solar heat building, based on our experience with the Vancouver courthouse, where we used an atrium as a passive solar heat sink. In the Sun Life buildings, there would have been six atriums, each six stories high, going up the whole height of each building, thirty-six or so stories. The atriums would have faced east and west so that they would have been heated from the east in the morning and the west in the evening, with the warm air circulated by thermostats."
—Erickson

bitterness. "It's really terrible. What comes out is not your design. Sawaber won't look at all like our conception. In Fintas, we have borrowed on the old Arab walled city with its narrow winding streets where you can always find shade, and the native market place, the *souk,* which has tiny stalls where the merchants sit on raised platforms with their merchandise. There are a lot of millionaires in Kuwait, for whom shopping is their main recreation. They can't even swim, because they are not allowed to go around in bathing suits."

"Our basic layout of clusters around a mosque has traditional gardens and cascades of water. A children's centre, the main couturiers—Balmain, Cardin, Yves St. Laurent, and so on, are at one end which is air-conditioned, and the *souk* at the other," he continued. "Everyone can walk around without coming into contact with cars. What appears to be a wall around the shopping centre is actually made up of parking garages."

VI

S *tunning.* was the word that came to my mind when I saw the interior of the New Massey Concert Hall in Toronto for the first time, in the spring of 1981. That was more than a year and a half before it was due to open officially in September, 1982. I arrived at the hall after the workmen had left for the day, and watched my own image approaching in the mirrored outside wall as I stepped over the construction barriers on the site. I was seeing just the basic glass and cement building, where only the interior glass walls of the lobby and the escalators had been installed.

In the auditorium of this new home for the Toronto Symphony Orchestra and for its forty-year-old companion, the Toronto Mendelssohn Choir, Erickson's architecture was exposed in a pure form that is never so clear once carpets, wooden stage, seats—and in this case a very elaborate acoustical ceiling and pipe organ—are in place. A massive circular stainless steel ring on the ceiling over my head was the only ornamentation.

The cement was a soft warm grey, in a colour that made me think of old silver. Everything was this silver grey cement; the orchestra pit, the cement steps where the orchestra seats would be placed and above them, small-sized cantilevered sections at different levels, convexly curved at the front, which are Erickson's concept of balconies. The convex curve, a useful device to scatter sound, was repeated in the cement walls in a flatter, elongated version that Erickson's staff have nicknamed "airplane wings." Whether through colour or spacing, or both, the auditorium seemed cosy and warm, far smaller than it is. Acting on a suggestion from Francisco Kripacz, Erickson has chosen the silver grey of this cement as his colour theme: grey carpet, silvery grey upholstered seats, grey fabric covering the lower part of the wall at the orchestra level, and of course, the grey of the structural cement wherever it is exposed.

Outside the auditorium are more variations of grey—stainless steel tubing for handrails, stainless steel doors polished to mirror shine; aluminium steel mullions—the technical term for visual divisions—that seal the joints of the mirrored glass shell which encases the whole building—with a mild colour change in the white exterior pipes that hold up the superstructure. The canopy that covers the hall is glass and steel—a tubular steel net covered in diamond-shaped panes that give a light transparency through which activities inside the hall can be seen at night. Colour has been saved for the concert hall ceiling, ranging from white and grey to scarlet, burgundy and deep purple.

"The Chairman of the Board of Directors of Massey Hall, Ed Pickering, told me in the beginning that the one thing he didn't like about modern architecture is the straight line that you never find in nature," Erickson said later, when I caught up with him in Vancouver. "So, very early in our designing, we started looking at solutions that reflected his desire to get away from the straight line. That is how the interior of the hall resulted in a plan that looks like the crab without legs you get in the eastern part of the United States—what do you call it?—a horseshoe crab."

"A concert hall is like a museum," he continued. "We built models of the

New Massey Hall, Toronto (1976). Interior during construction.

"Most architects are forced to do things acoustically that look fake, with a decorative treatment that is quickly dated. We wanted everything we did in Massey Hall to serve a purpose structurally, mechanically, theatrically."
—Erickson

New Massey Hall. Viewed during construction from CN Tower.

**New Massey Hall.
Model showing
canopy as
originally designed
by Erickson.**

**New Massey Hall.
Photograph of
completed
structure showing
altered canopy.**

seating and put a shell around it, and we
did the outside setting at the same time.
We went through thirty-two models to
establish the shape of Massey Hall and
to make sure the acoustics would be
correct for the shape of the building and
that the walls would relate to the seating
and ceiling. What I dislike about all
opera houses and concert halls is the
phony decorative patterns, usually full of
rectangles, produced by acoustic
treatment of walls. I like to see the bare
bones of a structure, with a quiet
background that lets the audience
supply most of the colour.''

Even the six-hundred-and-twenty-five-
thousand-dollar pipe organ for the new
hall, from the workshop of Gabriel Kney,
of London, Ontario, had been
constructed to Erickson's design and
colour scheme. Mr. Kney was planning
to build his organ with a classic wooden
case, and as Keith Loffler, the architect
in charge of Erickson's Toronto office,
described the situation, ''A case is a
very specialized thing, and he would
have every technical reason to want one
of wood, since the case is used to
reflect the sound from the pipes.'' With
five thousand two hundred and seven
pipes, the three-storey-tall organ is
highly visible above and behind the
orchestra. Erickson's overall design
called for a glass-enclosed section at
the bottom of the organ where the wires
and pulleys are located; the wires
connect to the keys, which he also
wanted lit while the organ was in use.
The rest of the case was to be panelled
with a glossy silver paint finish; actually
automotive enamel, which gives the
shining silver effect that Erickson was
seeking.

Opposite: New Massey Hall.

"Massey Hall is purely a concert hall and we have tried to maintain as much of the intimacy of the old one as possible. We have approximately the same seat count but more leg space."

—Erickson

"Mr. Kney is a very headstrong guy, and I could foresee problems," Loffler continued, "so I said to Arthur, 'You had better come to the meeting about the organ and be presented with the design.' Much to my amazement, Arthur not only came but basically approved, and then sure enough, a couple of months later, he said, 'Why don't we try to organize another meeting and try to change a few things.' Well, I knew that to get Kney to accept the glass-enclosed organ with silver-painted panelling was going to take a long process. Meeting by meeting he gradually came around. You can know what you want to achieve but it's a long process to get everyone thinking your way." The New Massey Hall organ is the ninety-fifth organ Mr. Kney has made, and the interior design has been left entirely to him; with pipes of wood and metal of his choice, palisander wood keys, a permanent console with mechanical action, a touch key system for stops, and a portable electronic console that can be used on the stage.

Erickson was not so lucky with the manufacturers who were to make the glass for the roof of the New Massey Hall. "The roof is not nearly as interesting as it was intended to be," Erickson said. "Originally it was a complex and beautiful shape, an ellipse transforming to a square. Our scheme called for two thousand different sizes of glass on the outside that were to be manufactured and set by computer. Unfortunately we were ahead of our time technically. The glass companies weren't up to it. The glass was to have been put in with silicone joints—no mullions. The Vancouver Courthouse

glass went in without mullions but nobody would do it in Toronto, it was considered too complicated—so now it's a rather clumsy roof. The original New Massey Hall roof would have been like a huge glass net but now we have a square and on it a circle, joined by a curved wall to a smaller circle at the top, a much stiffer profile. It would have been unique—and so elegant!"

"The whole hall is a shell within a shell; two completely independent concrete shells not even joined over one structure, with eight or ten feet between them, to keep all sound out," he continued. "The auditorium is thirty thousand square feet in area, eighty feet high, and has an audience capacity of twenty-eight hundred and seventy-five persons. The one thing I didn't want to do was get into enormous balconies, and that's where I got the idea of seating people in more intimate sections, in what we call 'pods'. The smallest seat about a dozen people, the larger ones from fifty to seventy-five, and the sections are at different levels, but two tiers of the pods go all the way around the hall and merge with seating behind the orchestra. When the choir is singing with the orchestra they are choir stalls, but otherwise I think of those seats as having high priority for students of music."

"The other thing is the ceiling," he went on with a slight smile, pulling a pad of paper towards him and drawing a large circle, which he began quickly filling in with fascinating-looking appendages. "In a hall, the ceiling is the one big surface and you really have to do something about it. Traditionally, opera houses are the most exciting. The great ones have ceilings worth looking up at when you're bored, but we didn't want to try a decorative treatment, which would be quickly dated, and we wanted everything in the hall to serve a purpose structurally. We thought we had to make the ceiling terribly important, but treat the rest of the hall as simply as possible. Our ceiling has many functions: air conditioning, lighting, heating that is fed in from the top (and very little of that because the audience does most of the heating), extra speaker systems for rock concerts and special arrangements to hear voice over the orchestra. But what is most interesting to me is the adjustable acoustical system in the ceiling. The acoustical experts wanted to be able to change the reverberation time of the hall according to the music being played; really, to be able to tune the hall, and they asked for an arrangement of absorptive adjustable materials with three settings for different kinds of music.''

The appendages he had been drawing now took on the form of long narrow tubes, as he continued talking. ''We hired Mariette Rousseau Vermette from Quebec, one of Canada's top fibre artists, who has worked on the curtains at Kennedy Centre in Washington, D.C. and at the opera house in Ottawa. She came up with acoustical banners in the form of tapestried cylinders five inches in diameter and eleven feet long; about four thousand, like a huge sunburst that radiates out from the centre of the hall. They are suspended from a structure we designed, a kind of stainless steel bicycle wheel that supports a catwalk for the special lighting and helps support the ceiling.''

I said that I had seen the wheel. ''The whole composition acts as the chandelier for the hall, and the banners fit in between all these cables and lights,'' Erickson added. ''I'd say that it's an art work of lighting, acoustical banners, structures, everything. A very complicated arrangement.''

Erickson's design responsibilities include not just the concert hall but an entire complex in Toronto slightly larger than Vancouver's civic centre, Robson Square. The ten acres of prime land in downtown Toronto was originally owned by the Marathon Realty Company, who wanted to put up office buildings. In return for rights to develop the south end with high-rise office structures with a density of a million square feet of office space, Marathon sold the east end to Massey Hall for a million dollars, a giveaway price, and

allocated the centre two-and-a-half acres for a park leased to the city for a dollar a year. This type of barter has become common now between municipalities and developers, as open land in cities becomes increasingly scarce and expensive.

Erickson sees the concert hall as the sculptured element of the park that lies between it and Marathon's buildings. The mirrored outer walls that encase the concert hall will be repeated in the office structures and presumably in those of a small recital hall in a space beside the concert hall that has been set aside for the future and landscaped in the meantime. Mirrors suit Erickson's perception of infinity and the mutability of life, and practically speaking, blend a structure with its surroundings by causing the mass to vanish into the reflecting outer landscape. Greenery is

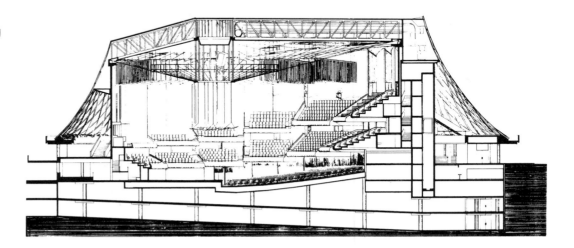

reflected in multiple images that add the illusion of more outdoor expanse in the kind of densely built up area that New Massey Hall is in.

The park design contains well known Erickson touches: at one end, a covered walkway in the form of a trellis, which will enable office workers to walk from the subway directly into the Marathon buildings; at the other end, a special, small sunken garden with a quiet reflecting pool filled with water lilies that concertgoers can reach by walking from the lobby to a balcony that overlooks it. The main feature of the park, however, is an amphitheatre at the west end, which when not in use becomes a garden with a waterfall. A few hours before a performance the waterfall is turned off, so the concrete steps can dry out and become seats. The amphitheatre has room for eight hundred people, and it is estimated that the surrounding park can hold another two to three thousand. The orchestra prefers playing indoors, but a cement shelf has been provided for them to come out from the hall to play on at ground level, facing the waterfall-turned-amphitheatre. A large restaurant has been planned to overlook the waterfall, which will have a covered walkway directly into the concert hall.

Only the orchestra and the personnel working there have eating facilities inside New Massey Hall, but this is an improvement over working conditions in Old Massey Hall. The players there have no place they can go even to rest except the basement, where there are a few tables, hat racks and lockers. In the new building they are well looked after, with shower rooms, changing rooms, offices

New Massey Hall. Interior looking out through glass wall.

"The concrete walls of Massey Hall are its actual skin, and you see the same wall inside as outside; but most places we build, we have to put on veneers. I don't like veneers although technically they are often necessary. Veneer is the second skin that covers a structure, and it seems to me to look like wallpaper. We have lost the technique, for instance, of using stone as anything but wallpaper, and I would have to start in a very small way to use it, on a house. It would be nice to do a stone house."
—Erickson

for both the Toronto Symphony
Orchestra and the Mendelssohn Choir,
and a library at stage level.

The red brick Old Massey Hall, which
opened in 1894, was a gift to Toronto
from the Massey family for whom it was
named, and has been declared an
historic site. Since it has never run at a
deficit, the Board of Governors, which is
the same for both New and Old Massey
Halls, are keeping it open for other
events, and plans to raise the money for
its renovation, when it finishes paying
bills on the forty-million-dollar new hall.
Toronto citizens have a great fondness
for ''the old lady of Shuter Street'' which
has nourished them culturally all their
lives, but they do not care for the wooden
seats in the second balcony, or for the
lack of air-conditioning which keeps it
closed in July and August. Its rather
Moorish, red black and gold auditorium,
like the new hall, is in the shape of a
horseshoe, with a similar seating
capacity of twenty-seven hundred and
sixty-five. ''It's ugly and weatherbeaten,''
its manager, Joseph Cartan, has
commented, ''but acoustically, it rates
very high, and Erickson came over at
least a dozen times and went over it.
Erickson spent a lot of time in Old
Massey Hall.''

Line Drawing

*''Line tells
everything. I've
always been a great
admirer of those
who could express
the world with a
simple line, like
Matisse or Picasso.
Once you go beyond
line to shadow and
texture, you lose the
wealth of inference
that a simple line
drawing has. It
begins to take on a
reality which often
doesn't suggest the
possibilities that
are there.''*
—Erickson

VII

American cities were perhaps the first cities to show in their most intensively used urban cores a desolating impersonality as if no creature but a machine had made them. But this was also their vitality . . . . The thrust of **modern architecture was launched with** the development unique to America of purely utilitarian space.'' Erickson said this in a speech at Harvard University in April, 1980. In July, 1980, he made the same statement again, at Washington State University in Seattle, one week after he won the design competition for the biggest architectural project he has ever had in North America: the redevelopment of five city blocks in the middle of Los Angeles.

Obviously the sad condition of American cities has been lurking both in his conscious and superconscious thoughts for years, if the words he uses to describe urban America in his speeches are any indication: *ugly; chaotic sprawl; wastelands of parked cars; sunless spaces between towering edifices.* Because he is an optimist he usually ends with the plea that ''we must think of our cities as places to live in and enjoy, rather than places to work in and escape.'' Being an activist, he must have long ago decided to do something about it when the time was ripe. Since the completion of Vancouver's city centre in 1979, when his imaginative approach to urban design became widely known, his talents have been sought for everything from simple neighbourhood siting to the colossus in Los Angeles on Bunker Hill.

The simple siting involved a two-month land-use study of three hundred and fifty acres along one of the last undeveloped tracts of coastline in Southern California, between Newport

Beach and Laguna Beach below Los Angeles. The Irvine family, who own the tract, originally had a ten-thousand acre ranch there. California has a coastal commission that protects land from certain forms of development, and a series of earlier plans for the site had been rejected. Although the Irvine Company had set aside a large portion of the land for a public park, it wanted to retain some of the choice parts for eighty-five estate houses on two-to-five acre lots, with space for swimming pools and tennis courts on each lot, and to erect hotels, a convention hall and retail stores on the land as well.

Erickson was hired to show the company how to use the landscape, space houses, and design roads so that whatever was built would have identity, be attractive, have a portion of the spectacular view, and together with the other buildings have the least possible impact on the natural beauty of the coast. The contour of the land took the form of a series of ridges and gullies running perpendicular to the coast. Erickson suggested that the gullies be planted with native vegetation and that the houses be placed on the sides of the gullies, far enough out to get the view but not prominently displayed in what would normally be prime locations. Access roads would be in the gullies. Two small hotels were placed at one end of the site, and the three large ones, one containing the convention hall, were at the other end, along the highway together with the retail stores. The California Coastal Commission approved Erickson's plan, ending a history of unsuccessful proposals that went back fifteen years.

California Centre, Bunker Hill, Los Angeles (1980).

Bunker Hill

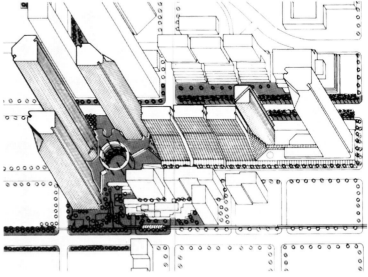

In 1911, the Province of British Columbia bought one hundred acres of land, directly across the inner harbour from downtown Victoria, from the Songhees Indian tribe living there, for $755,753.75. The purchase price included a new reserve for the Songhees in nearby Esquimault, a ten-thousand-dollar-payment to each family for moving, and the removal and reinterment of their dead. The Songhees Peninsula, as it is still known, was designated for industry but never used, and in 1981, Erickson was asked by the Provincial Government to make an urban design for the whole peninsula redefining the street system, and outlining phased residential development. Erickson regards this as an extension of an earlier harbour plan he did for Victoria, but this time he was given an additional project: a twelve-million dollar housing development covering some five and a half acres. Fifty units are designated for senior citizens, and a hundred houses for families, arranged in a kind of town mews, to conform with Victoria's view of itself as a bit of Olde England.

In Vancouver, Marathon Realty wanted Erickson to design two buildings on waterfront land. Erickson feels that whatever goes up there should be a "gateway to the city", and his plans call for one of his atrium spaces, a glass-enclosed plaza one hundred and forty feet high; a landscaped, all-weather "place" well-suited to a city in which an umbrella is standard equipment for all outdoor ventures. The glass gallery lies between two pylon-like buildings that make the site economically viable—two angular faceted towers, one over thirty

storeys tall, the other about sixteen, both flat on the atrium side. The glassed-in plaza, surrounded by restaurants, will serve as an entertainment centre for noon-hour concerts, with night clubs and other evening activities woven into the pattern of atrium life. "What you'll see if you come into the harbour by ship is a crystal vaulted gallery that you can look through between the buildings, which pedestrians can also look through from the site to see the water," Erickson has explained. "I've suggested the scheme of marketing be focussed on Orient and Pacific trade, with a Japanese hotel and first class Chinese and Japanese restaurants."

Erickson's multi-purpose complex in Seattle, Washington, derives its name, Harbor Steps, from a monumental flight of stairs, sixty feet wide with a fountain in the centre, that he has designed as the major pedestrian access to the waterfront from the central business district. The thoroughfare of steps is on alignment with Seattle's old University Street, and another street, Post Alley, connects the site with two other important points, the Pike Street produce market and the historic Pioneer Square. A pair of slim office towers, with art deco stepped sides, thirty storeys high, are to frame the steps on either side, and two other buildings, a seven-storey, two hundred-room hotel, and a terraced apartment structure six or seven storeys tall will be introduced to the two-acre site. One old building that Erickson thought had sufficient historic merit to be preserved will remain, coincidentally called The Erickson Building. Post Alley, a third the width of University Street, will become the

primary pedestrian and retail street, but the design emphasis will be on the steps, where the special shops and more elegant restaurants will be located. By current Erickson standards, the Seattle site, originally four short city blocks, one hundred thousand square feet of land in all, is a small area, but he expects that with what it offers, it will be a focal point in revitalizing Seattle's rundown central waterfront district.

One sunny Saturday morning I stopped in to talk with Erickson in his Vancouver house about the design for the billion-dollar, five-block urban redevelopment project on Bunker Hill in Los Angeles. Bunker Hill played an important role in the city's early history and the site is the last major piece of urban development left in the downtown. Its placement is strategic. It is near the financial heart of the city. Even closer are the clutch of government buildings that comprise the Civic Centre, from which a park-like area leads west to the Music Centre, whose three theatres provide a focal point for the cultural activities of Los Angeles. Directly south is Pershing Square, where that renowned city landmark, The Hotel Biltmore, is ensconced. To the north is the plaza, "El Pueblo de Los Angeles," now a state park and tourist mecca, where the town was founded by the Spaniards in 1781. Also in the vicinity are the old Grand Central Market, Little Tokyo, and Chinatown.

Erickson's design for the eleven-acre L-shaped site contains three large office towers, the tallest fifty-two storeys, adjacent to the Los Angeles business core, and a four-hundred room hotel one block from the Music Centre. In between are three residential buildings, side by side, with a total of eight hundred apartments. The competition called for a museum of contemporary art as well, which Erickson "slotted into a notch" across the lower six floors of all three apartment buildings, with glass walls so that people passing in the park or on Grand Avenue beyond could catch a glimpse of what was being shown. The interweave of the museum with the housing and shopping reflects a central theme of all his urban work, one for which he has added a new word to his vocabulary: linkage. "It's the interconnection, the interrelationship of the parts of the city that had been separated by the mechanistic thinking that began with the Renaissance," Erickson says. However, he has had to revise his placement of the projected museum to conform with the wishes of its independent board of directors, who wanted a free-standing structure and hired Japanese architect Arata Isozaki to design it.

When I walked into Erickson's garden he was sitting in a chair on the marble slab by the pool, looking a bit tired but otherwise fit. I asked him how he felt about the direction his work had been taking since our first meeting several years ago, and he sat back a few minutes, contemplating. Then he said, "I'm in my third phase. Complexes. Consortiums. They really take me onto the international stage. I think of my first period as early house design, and my second as Simon Fraser University right up to the present. I don't know what this third phase is going to lead to eventually. With this project in California, I'll be looking more and more

to the States. I might even be moving there and commuting here, although I'll always keep my Vancouver office."

"The project of course is prodigious," he went on. "With six groups who had to be brought together under one management, we had to create a new joint venture office in Los Angeles. We didn't even know each other! Three architectural firms are involved, and we would only go in if our firm was responsible for the design. One of these other firms has the task of production drawings, and a third, the management. The interesting thing is, everyone says it's an enormous project and it is, but for the amount of headache and concern it will cause, with all the expense, what comes into our office is relatively little. So you think: how can I afford it? With all that commuting and renting a house there and so on?"

"What sold my design to the Community Development Association of Los Angeles was my use of the spaces between the buildings, not just as left-over spaces, but as a green park," he continued. "The competition asked for two acres of open space and we gave them a little more than six acres on the ground in park. Then we extended the green even up the high rise buildings. Each office tower appears in our plan as a shimmering glass form in two slipped triangles joined by landscaped balconies that go up the full height of the building."

"At the competition stage of design, the buildings themselves were indicated in a very general, abstract way," he said, after a pause. "No one was expected to produce architecture. Our design was more an urban concept of

the downtown. What we did with the open space on the ground was to provide a lavish park like the green parks that you can go through in the dense part of London. You can walk from Kensington to Picadilly Circus almost entirely through parks. Our plan gives Los Angeles a continuous park which extends within a block of both the Music Centre park and Pershing Square. All through the park there will be dense plantings; feather palms, canopied sycamores, redwoods, lacy jacarandas, wisteria, bougainvillea, roses, *everything!*"

He sat forward, talking rapidly. "The park crossing from Grand Avenue to Hill Street on the bottom of the L drops sixty feet, or six storeys in height, going through a number of levels. Our idea is to put a reconstructed version right there of the funicular railway called Angel's Flight that used to run up and down Bunker Hill in the early days, and an historical museum beside it to create linkage with the city's past. The uppermost park level will form a promenade from the hotel to the office towers. Pedestrians can progress through gardens traditional to the Hispanic past of Los Angeles: a garden featuring scents, such as jasmine and orange; a water garden of fountains and runnels; and a sculpture garden. They arrive finally at a circular plaza with an outdoor performance area which provides a sophisticated setting where all kinds of performing artists—ballet dancers, pop singers, quartets, and so on—can be exposed to the public. It will be an informal lunch area in the daytime and like a cabaret at night. In inclement or chilly weather, a canopy will unfurl to protect the stage and the audience. We also celebrate the central role Los Angeles played in the film world with a twelve-theatre cinema complex. Eventually the cinemaplex could be tied with a film library and serve as a museum of film.''

''Seven or eight dozen shops and restaurants will border the park, and I should mention the idea we have for eating,'' he said. ''Food is a new development almost a cult in America, and we are thinking that the produce and all the appliances to produce good food could be sold in the same shop as the restaurant, like it is done in the Les Halles market in Paris. There you see the food in trays, displayed in front of the restaurant, and you can either eat it there, or buy it to take home!''

He was silent for a moment, then said, ''As I see it, the Bunker Hill project will provide a multi-faceted cultural centre through five blocks of the city that is unprecedented anywhere in the world. Los Angeles grew as a collection of scattered settlements, eventually linked by a broad framework of freeways; a vast collection of suburbs. I think it can still grow into a single great city by blending what began as residential villages and places of work and entertainment, the way London did. I view our project as the key in establishing this pattern, tying together the disparate strands of government and cultural centres, popular markets, ethnic communities and business developments so that it becomes the centre for all these other centres. Making connections.''

Erickson put his head back and closed his eyes, enjoying the warmth of

Air Defense Headquarters, Riyadh, Saudi Arabia (1979). Model photograph.

"A . . . military headquarters building was restricted in height to no more than 30 metres, and yet it was to have some visual importance. So we dug 30 metres into the ground to get a building twice as high. From one side it looks as if it is part of the desert; there are no windows, only walls that step up from the desert floor. As you approach it you begin to see down into a court that is a kind of oasis around which are arranged the mirrored boxes of the offices looking into this inner court . . . We found that the offices reflecting the oasis give an enormous sense of cool green in the centre . . . "
—Erickson

Below: Rendering of Air Defence Headquarters showing V.I.P. entrance.

the sun. "Have you heard about our work in the Middle East?" he asked. Knowing he has a long list of projects there that changes almost daily, I asked for an update. "We've just signed a contract in Iraq for the redevelopment of the east bank of the Tigris River in Baghdad," he said. "It's a strip a little more than two miles long in an area called Abu Nuwas, named after a famous eighth-century Baghdad poet. It was one of the first parts of the city to expand beyond the old walls in the early nineteen-twenties. We have to look at the historical buildings to see what is to be preserved, and at the site's potential for recreation, housing, institutional and commercial purposes. It already is an entertainment and restaurant area, and the government is looking for it to be a kind of showplace for a future Arab meeting."

He opened his eyes. "In the Middle East, in the desert regions of the earth, I discovered that another language emerged and that I was fumbling with a new form, desert architecture. I am being forced to learn about walls as a protection from light and the extremes of heat. I must also acquire new attitudes towards space, which in Islamic architecture is static, with no movement towards a goal as it is in the West. Islamic space is for separate enjoyment; each space is a sanctuary and it matters not how or whether it connects to the next open space. In the desert there is nothing but sand and sky and the nakedness of the earth exposed to relentless sun or the freezing empty space of the nights full of stars. Architecture provides escape from the hostile environment to a cool tranquil interior where there is a courtyard with

splashing fountains and gardens, while the exterior is an austere bulwark against the elements."

"I find that I am very much a part of the American northwest tradition, where weak light demands large glass areas that should adjoin a wall or floor so that light washes into a room without glare. Post and beam frees the wall to do this and that's why it's so intrinsic to my design. In the Northwest, there is nothing more depressing than the glaring grey light coming from a window punched into a wall. I love unbroken wall spaces. I cannot bear to punch holes in them, and this marks me. So I am experimenting."

"It's a fascinating experience for me, opening untried horizons," he went on. "In the Sawaber housing project in Kuwait, I tried stacking apartments that were really enclosed villas with an outside courtyard in staggered offset, so that light came in vertically, with small shuttered windows in outer walls for looking out. In Medina, we put a shopping centre under the housing, with a glass roof which looked up into shaded space. In a military headquarters we arranged mirrored offices hung from a concrete shelter around an inner court like an oasis, whose reflection gave an enormous sense of cool green in the centre. In a ministry in Riyadh, my first attempt to deal with light and shade in an office building, I placed the building as an umbrella over the site, with light shafts decreasing in size in steps to small openings, bringing the light into the gardens below. We fronted the raised office block with pierced screens, which is a very arbitrary way of dealing with the sun."

"We'll be working for years on our

Saudi Arabian projects," he said. "We are in so many different groups. For example, King Abdul Aziz University, for twenty thousand students, involves a consortium of five firms and would cost somewhere between one and two billion dollars. It is our master plan, and if all goes well we're responsible for fifteen per cent of the work—the central plaza and administration building, the main library, the student centre, a museum, an aquarium, an auditorium, and half the student and faculty housing. For the projected King Faisal Air Force Academy, our design includes academic spaces, a library, dining facilities, extensive laboratories, a physical education department, housing for the fifteen hundred cadets on the site, and a main mosque for the air base community of two thousand people."

"All this has required years of intensive negotiations but I have kept out of all that," he added. "I didn't have the time. I don't want to go to meetings and I have no involvement until we start designing. I hardly know who works for me. It is a great disadvantage to a client, I suppose, that I'm not running the office or deciding who's employed. But each office has to be effective as a team. My offices consult me on projects as much as possible, and I'm involved in *all* the design. That's what I enjoy. That's why I'm in it. That's why I'm hired."

It was time to go. He walked me to the gate, and as I left he said, "I'll still be in Vancouver on Monday. Meet me in the office at four and I'll take you to see the courthouse. Then I'd like to show you the new Anthropology Museum at U.B.C."

VIII

Actually, Erickson runs his offices by not running them. The two main offices have separate directors, with a single comptroller supervising all financial matters. The whole operation has become increasingly complex with each international involvement. Erickson delegates everything but design to his staff, cultivating for himself a physical and spiritual remoteness that protects him from getting involved in other people's problems. His regular weekly absences from his offices in both Vancouver and Toronto often extend to many weeks when he is conferring with clients in, say, Saudi Arabia, and he takes a Christmas "holiday," often in an architectural area new to him. This narrows his role in humdrum office routine to frequent long-distance telephone calls, or telecopier transmittals, and all but the most urgent problems are solved by phone or telecopy consultations. "He generally has the idea for the design right in the beginning and then spends an enormous amount of time rationalizing it," an architect who used to work for him said. Erickson is never quite satisfied, however, with what he has done, leading to a process of ongoing change that Keith Loffler calls "creative procrastination." Erickson never stops working, and is apt to arrive in Vancouver from Toronto on a Friday night with a better, and sometimes entirely different, design for a project on which weeks or months of detailed work has been done. Then he expects his staff to pursue with him over the weekend the quest for the perfect design, which he knows does not exist but for which he feels compelled to strive.

Erickson employs anywhere from

thirteen to one hundred architects, depending upon the work in progress. His quietly efficient secretary, Lillian Ketola, has the onerous task of arranging his airline reservations, which he always changes—usually a number of times, a custom that has worn out several travel agents. The whole staff is on a first-name basis—a system that not only eliminates the need for Erickson to remember last names but gives the office an informal atmosphere. His office also makes the elaborate arrangements for the parties he loves to give, although he has been giving them with less and less frequency. An Erickson party is a dramatic and memorable performance, featuring exotic food, live musicians, ballet dancers, and candles that he sets out himself, in glass holders in the trees, transforming his garden into a shadowy, flickering world of beauty. He used to do the cooking himself for small dinners, but he needs the whole day for it and no longer has the time. A typical menu might include a cold sour-cherry soup, a whole salmon cooked with preserved ginger in a pastry shell, and a deboned whole chicken stuffed with spinach, pistachio nuts, and coriander, and covered with a yogurt sauce. He participated in a cooking contest in Toronto at a benefit ball in 1977 against eight other "celebrity chefs": the then Mayor of Toronto, David Crombie; John Craig Eaton of Eaton's Department Stores; two ballet stars, Karen Kain and Frank Augustyn; a hockey player; Richard Rohmer, the writer and lawyer; and the owners of a local TV station. The judges, members of the Canadian Chefs Association, restaurant owners, and the French Canadian gourmet Mme. Jehane Benoit, pronounced his *salmon en chemise* "elegant, but simple," and awarded it the first prize.

Erickson prides himself on his even temper, and he has rarely been known to lose it in the office, but one thing is guaranteed to infuriate him: the loss of his baggage after a flight, which is a fairly common occurrence. He has lost five full suits of clothing made in his favourite city, Rome, and numerous other items, and now he boards planes clutching all irreplaceables. "I get into a white fury at airports. I become quite unrecognizable," he says. "Losing baggage is a severe interruption of my schedule, and when it happens I immediately call the president of the airline." Once in a plane and settled into a window seat, however, he pulls out a sketch pad, architectural plans, or writing paper and has three or four blissful hours of uninterrupted concentration. He finds the three-hour jet lag between his two Canadian offices bracing. "Routine of any kind is bad for the health," he is fond of saying. "If I'm too long in a place, I become stale, or it becomes stale, or we both do. Planes are wonderful!"

The offices of Arthur Erickson Architects, on Laurel Street in Vancouver, are reached by crossing one of several bridges from the business centre over an inlet called False Creek. The three-storey building they occupy, which resembles a warehouse, is windowless on three sides. Its focal point is an enormous two-storey interior studio topped by a roof that, looked at from below, appears to be floating. I am accustomed now to Erickson's floating

Head office of Arthur Erickson Associates, Vancouver. View of main studio area.

"The cement wall at the end was open at one time, with an outdoor pool, but we took in the space as a part of the office when we needed more room. It's a very pleasant place to work."
—Nick Milkovich, architect

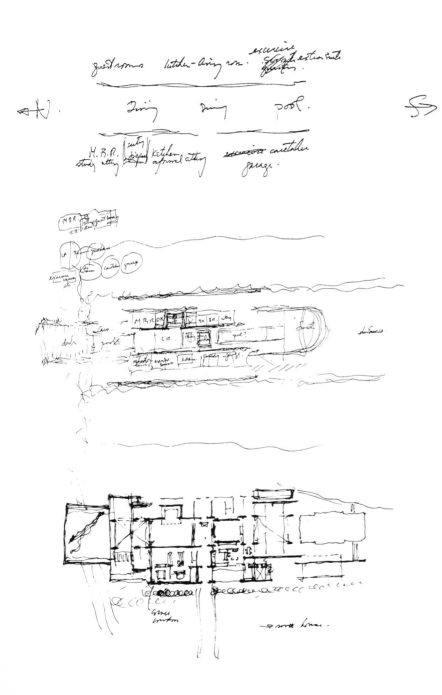

Bagley Wright house, Seattle (1977). Series of Erickson sketches showing evolution of design.

"When the human mind has a picture, it's very hard to change, so in thinking of the form for a building it's important to prevent having the picture as long as possible, and only after all the information has been gathered. After the first analysis we build a model of the site, and then we put block models on it to see the best organization. At that point we usually discuss the project with our client—a government, or company, or individual, to find out whether we have missed any information. Then we build a series of models, each larger as we begin to understand the structure or complex of buildings. Between the first model, a general massing model, and successive models, we begin discussing structural methods and finishing materials, which usually become obvious."

—Erickson

illusions, and a second, harder look reveals the roof to be supported by four huge pillars of rough-sawn Douglas fir, with struts two-thirds of the way up branching out like tree limbs. The walls surrounding the roof rise above it, and light washes down through the intervening space, which is spanned by almost invisible skylights. The studio is filled with drafting tables and with growing plants being tested for future use in Erickson buildings, and though there is a low hum from several dozen busy young people moving about or sitting at their work, it gives the impression of a quiet, airy garden.

I stopped in the studio to talk to Bing Thom, the firm's projects director until the spring of 1981, when he left to set up his own office in Vancouver. A small compact man in his late thirties, he is a third-generation Chinese Canadian who happens to have been born in Hong Kong. He and Erickson still have a separate partnership for the work they would like some day to get in China. Some years ago, they conducted a week of seminars in Peking for Chinese city planners and architects. Planning for tourist travel in China, the updating of building techniques and materials, and Erickson's own methods of arriving at designs for buildings were the main topics, with Erickson using his own slides of good and bad examples of tourist development to illustrate his points. Since then, the Chinese government has sent an architect from Shanghai to work in Erickson's office.

Bing Thom spent fifteen years with Erickson and was once his student. Looking around the office, I was curious about the "consistent chaos" which was not visible here. He laughed. "The chaos involves unimportant details. On important things, Arthur is well organized, with a feeling for priorities. The designing is Arthur's but he is still a teacher, with an evolutionary approach and the ability to listen. I have never heard him say, 'Do this because I want it, or like it.' Some people say working with Arthur is like playing the game of go, where you make a move and Arthur makes a move. Winning over a person's heart takes a lot of time—and projects here continue for two or three, even eight years, so your heart *has* to be in it. It is important that people he can work with be brought in when they are young, and Arthur accepts the fact that we grow up and fly on our own. Each project is started with a small team of architects —Arthur relates more easily to a few people—and together they set the ground rules and the basic direction. They all go away and think and do sketches, including Arthur. Then they come back together and lay the sketches on the table, throw out some, keep others. Then he goes away and they work on the project."

"Arthur approaches architecture the way a sculptor approaches clay," Thom continued. "He looks at a building from the outside in, the way it reacts to climate and terrain, and from the inside out, the way it's used and the way the light comes in. There is a strong Asian influence on the West Coast, and he understands that and expresses it. Many of his structures are like pavilions, with roofs and columns but few walls. Our climate is mild but damp, so all we need is an umbrella, and, where many architects' tendency is to nestle against

the ground, his approach is to stand above the rain and let the light come in and get you out of bed. In our mists and greyish light, you need strong buildings. He preserves the human scale by breaking up their edges with trellises or wooden grills."

Thom looked at his watch and stood up. "Arthur is a perfectionist," he said. "Just before a presentation, everyone usually does the whole thing over to make it just right, and everybody stays up all night. He reminds me of a kid running down a beach and picking up pebbles and always stopping to get more—trying to pick up that last pebble." Thom excused himself, saying he had an appointment. I descended a short flight of stairs at one side of the studio to a corridor giving on to glass-walled conference rooms. I could see Erickson and several young men seated at a table examining a model.

Around a corner, past a small library, and up another flight of stairs, I was directed through a heavy door of rough fir into Erickson's office and sat down to wait for him. A grey stream of daylight came down from the same unseen skylights that illuminated the studio, which was next to his office. The small room was otherwise windowless, with white walls, on which hung several handsome modern prints, among which I recognized a Joseph Albers and a Gordon Smith. An eclectic assortment of books on art, architecture, and horticulture occupied shelves covering two sides of the room, along with several framed diplomas and honourary degrees, and on a top shelf was a dusty bronze bust of George Vancouver, the explorer, with a Band-Aid over one eye.

Erickson's desk was a simple white shelf extending the length of the wall opposite the door, and beneath it was a second shelf, of cubbyholes filled with rolled-up drawings. Several folders and a delicate green ficus plant on top of the desk were reflected by mirrors at each end which extended to the ceiling and carried image after image: an indoor version of the Erickson endless vista.

While I was looking at the framed blue cancelled check for fifty thousand dollars from the Royal Bank which was propped up on a shelf, Erickson walked in. "I didn't have enough money to pay for parking my car when I went into the banquet for that award," he said, laughing. "I told the garage attendant, 'If you'll just wait until I come out, I'll have fifty thousand dollars.'" He sat down, turned his chair around toward me, and leaned back in his favourite position, hands behind his head, feet on his desk, and shut his eyes. I thought, 'He has gone to sleep or into some kind of a trance,' but he opened his eyes and said, "We don't have a design methodology and we *do* have a design methodology. I suppose a certain amount of order is good, but I've

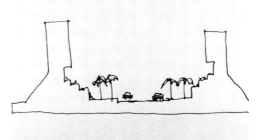

Bunker Hill

resisted it.'' He sighed. ''I'm the worst-organized person. I have no memory of what happened the day or week before, and have to have a note whether to turn right or left or where to go or why or whom I am meeting. Physically, I don't think I can keep it all in my head, so I have found the best method is to keep nothing in my head and be briefed. I have asked myself, 'What does a client want? For me to work on his project? Or to be at all the meetings where I am not really necessary?' What my clients are asking for is my design input, and by avoiding other involvement I save myself for that. The day of the person who has a central idea and enforces it is over, although there will always be a demand, in a rather limited area, for the architect who is an artist with a unique vision. Many of our multi-million dollar jobs are so big they *have* to be joint ventures or consortiums—Massey Hall, the Bank of Canada, Fintas, Bunker Hill, Saudi Arabia—but we won't go into a project unless we have the final say in design. We *have* to be in charge of design.''

''For any large project, we build a model of the site, and I usually find my ideas crystallizing in a conversation with somebody,'' he continued. ''An idea that has been cooking on the back burner comes forward in a challenging situation. Studying ahead of time closes my mind, which needs my whole life experience to be kept open. If you burden your mind with facts, you narrow down your field of information—eliminate all the input that could come from your superconscious. In any basic effort today, you need a full complement of minds. I am aware of the visual effect

of every detail, and I happen to have the kind of mind that relates details to a larger context, so I hire someone who sees the grains of sand on the beach. I often tell my people I can't read, because I have a completely visual memory. I do think when you develop your visual sense the others atrophy. I ask that things be presented to me visually and that detailed information be reduced to simple statements illustrated by diagrams. When all the statements are brought together, you begin to absorb the sense of an over-all design.''

He brought his feet down, and began twirling a felt pen on his desk. ''I suppose I learned from my mother and grandfather and from my travels, which gave me objectivity, not to accept any status quo, so I can remove something from its cultural context and see it alone. I challenge everything. I do the conceptual sketches, and we work a lot from models. The people here in my office study things thoroughly, so if I'm off base they can correct me. Although the system may seem chaotic, things are very much under control, with the office having priority on my time. I am deeply involved in all the projects and give decisions at every level—from construction involving millions of dollars to someone's bathroom tile. Sometimes I realize an hour later that I haven't thought about something carefully enough, and have to go back. Most firms analyze a client's needs and arrive at a solution quickly. I always start out with the approach—which may be a little Oriental—that we have no ideas about *anything*. If anyone said to me 'I have an idea for a building,' I would immediately be suspicious, because in my terms

that's not architecture. You can't transplant solutions from one place to another. Buildings are a response to specific requirements, the most fundamental being the locale. Ideas almost always arise in consultation with the client, and the design is a slow process of evolution. The important thing is that you question. The client comes in with a set of traditional ideas, and by questioning this you take him further in his own idea than he would have thought conceivable. We keep all possibilities open until practically the last moment—a frustrating, sometimes terrifying experience for the person working for me. Sometimes it even makes *me* nervous. But somehow it always comes together.'' He stood up and said, ''Let's go!''

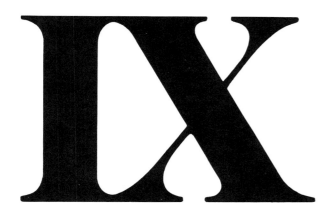

IX

On the way out of his office, we stopped in the studio at a model, set on a long trestle, of the three-block complex in the centre of Vancouver, which is still known around the office as 51-61-71—the numbers on the official properties map of the city blocks involved. ''Since 1958, I have had three go-arounds at studies for the city of Vancouver on transit, harbours, development of various whole areas, and a limited subway, which could tie together all the shopping centres already in existence,'' Erickson said. ''51-61-71 is a whole section of the city, and with it I think that Vancouver, which has been an adolescent, has grown up. A city matures when the citizens flock to the centre, not for work but for pleasure. We have linked three blocks together into a major civic centre and public square for the city, with tree plantings to give a boulevard effect, and provided a pedestrian mall with only buses allowed through.''

As my eyes adjusted to the model, I saw that here in miniature were the plazas, buildings, terraced parks over partly sunken offices lit by skylights, a forest with walking trails, waterfalls— the whole traversed with ''stramps'' (his name for ramps that weave in and out of wide-spaced stairs), along which I have often walked in a parklike atmosphere that is totally enjoyable. Erickson's hand rested briefly on a block-long building covered by a slanting canopy of glass, easily recognizable as the most striking addition to Vancouver's skyline. ''Block 71, the new courthouse,'' he said. His hand moved towards Block 51, lightly touching a spot in front of the old courthouse. ''My signature—a mound, to provide a soft transition between the old and the new.''

It was still early enough in the

**Courthouse—
Robson Square
Complex,
Vancouver (1973)**

*"Thirty per cent of
the civic centre is in
plants, and it is a
city park. We like to
refer to it as a
metropolitan forest,
although it is not as
high as in nature,
because of soil
depth limitations.
The whole system is
monitored by
computers in the
basement of '61,'
for fertilizer and
water, and is divided
into zones. If natural
rain requires a
change, special
cards can override
the regular orders."*
—Cornelia
Oberlander

**Robson Square.
Falls over office
window.**

*"People are
encouraged to walk
in the waterfalls by
having steps that go
right down to the
little lakes beneath."*
—Bing Thom

**Opposite:
Courthouse
pedestrian hall
showing truss roof
interior.**

day that traffic was light and we
talked casually as he drove. "I made a
tour of courthouses before we started
designing, as one does," he said. "At
Osgoode Hall in Toronto, I was alarmed
by the number of keys everyone carried.
Then, inadvertently, we were locked into
the detention cell of one of the courts. I
was shocked that in a modern country
we have cages like animal cages to hold
prisoners—which shows my naivete. No
matter how innocent a person might be,
he would feel guilty by the time he got
into court. So, when I came back, I said,
'I will open up the corridors, so anyone
coming in can see where he has to go.' I
was also influenced by the casual
remark of a distinguished judge and
good friend that an ancient British
custom of 'dispensing justice in the
street' appealed to him. I thought, 'Why
not open up our corridors to the street,
and then justice will be part of the
education of our citizens!' The
courtrooms are screened from the
public by plantings and solid walls, but
a pedestrian way goes past with public
access to them. The space is large
enough to hold gatherings of six
hundred people."

He dropped me off at "51", the old
courthouse-art gallery end of Robson
Square, while he parked the car, and I
walked over to the east wall of that
building to look at six London plane trees
Bing Thom had urged me to see. They
were rich leafy healthy-looking trees, in
sharp contrast to the wispy sunset
maples that surround the site. When
Erickson was planning 51-61-71, he
wanted to create a major downtown
park with beautiful treed boulevards
along the three blocks. He envisioned a

**Courthouse—
Robson Square.
View of "stramps."**

*"Steps are not
just for moving up
and down but act
as a kind of a
theatre where you
have the observed
and the observers
intermingling."*
—Erickson

small Champs Elysée in Vancouver, a
canopy of trees for people to walk
through, which would make a strong
edge around the project. Then he heard
that three hundred plane trees ordered
for the World's Fair in Spokane,
Washington, in 1974, and never used,
were available. What a once-in-a-
lifetime opportunity! He urged the
provincial government to buy them,
which it did, and after the trees had been
growing several years, first in an Oregon
nursery, then in one nearer home, the
city of Vancouver's engineers ruined his
dream by refusing to plant them. "The
engineers said the plane trees would be
too costly to maintain and all Erickson's
considerable persuasive powers could
not make them change their minds,
although many large cities have plane
trees, including Vancouver itself. The
city engineers refused those trees in
retribution for my closing Robson Street
where it bisects the site to all vehicles
except buses, against their wishes,"
Erickson said later. "The maples they
planted instead have aphids and require
spraying, but there are no aphids on our
plane trees. No disease on ours."
Gordon Shrum suddenly sold the rest of
the plane trees to the city of Victoria for
a waterfront promenade, without
consulting Erickson; all but those
Erickson planted within the site "to
show what the city might have had, in
twenty years."

I looked at the broad-leafed plane
trees, eloquently verdant in the shadow
of the courthouse wall, and quickly
walked away. I descended the
"stramps", alternating between steps
and ramps, down to the restaurant area
where Erickson and I had agreed to

meet, by a Viennese coffee shop. I looked around at the people who were strolling past or sitting on the benches or steps, and watched a boy whiz down the stramps on a skateboard. I thought about Erickson's remark that Vancouver had grown up when citizens flocked to its centre for pleasure. At the end of September, 1979, soccer fans held an impromptu homecoming celebration in Robson Square for Vancouver's professional soccer team, the Vancouver Whitecaps, after they had beaten the New York and Tampa, Florida teams for the North American championship. The spontaneous gathering had filled the outdoor plaza for the first time since its official opening, doing great damage to the new plantings. Crowds tramped on the shrubbery and small boys climbed into the fledgling trees for a better view of the victorious athletes, bringing down showers of leaves and branches; a small price, Erickson's landscape architect in charge of the planting, Cornelia Oberlander, feels for what she and many others regard as the baptism of Robson Square as a "people's place."

Erickson arrived now, walking lightly down the stramps. "I hate to visit like this, I see all the wrong things that should be corrected," he remarked as we started towards the central plaza on Block 61, where the provincial offices are located. We passed a large flat glass surface through which offices underneath could be clearly seen, and a look of real pain crossed Erickson's face. "Water from a whole waterfall should be spilling over those offices," he said, as we rapidly moved on. "This place should look beautiful. I don't want

to go inside there now. The only interiors we did anyway are the courtrooms."

I had already been through the provincial offices, over which we were still walking. Windowless rooms, even if there is light coming from above, do not appeal to me, and Erickson was obviously as eager to move on to the new courthouse as I was. We hurried along, climbing a flight of concrete steps into what appeared briefly to be an enclosed garden that by some strange sleight of hand seemed apart from the surrounding city; the path curved away and seemed to disappear. Turning in the direction from which we had come for a moment, the old courthouse was distantly visible through the shrubbery and trees. "You are looking at a neoclassical building through an eighteenth-century garden," Erickson said. "We are at the top level of 61 here. The offices for visiting provincial ministers and the premier—right now the crown attorneys are using them—are right behind us, hidden by plantings. On the level above us, the roof of their offices holds the large reflecting pond that feeds the three waterfalls below us. I see that they are turned on now," he added, and smiled. There was a pleasant sound of rushing water, and I could see cascades of waters flowing downward. We were surrounded by lush growth of Japanese maples, pine trees and white azaleas. "It's something else, isn't it?" he said softly. "This is called the quiet area—it's for resting and thinking." He pointed upward to planters filled with rose bushes, although they were not in bloom. "A curtain of pale white roses comes down over this wall. Rosa Wichuriana, the Memorial Rose.

One feels so secluded here."

We walked across a small bridge over the street below. Around us were planters filled with yew and laurel shrubs, so that the area scarcely seemed like what it was: a passage to a destination. "Where possible, we have tried to make indigenous plantings to reintroduce into the city what was once there," he said.

I was so intrigued by this tiny parkland that I wasn't aware until we went through a double glass door that we had come into the new courthouse; into the great hall with its enormous slanting glass canopy.

Erickson stood quietly beside me, as if he too was absorbing the grand scheme of this interior for the first time; the lofty space-frame of glass laced with white painted steel that rises seven storeys, its sloping glass surface a hundred and fifty feet wide. From the main floor of the great hall, three sets of grand stairs ascend from gallery to gallery until they arrive at the top.

New Courthouse, Vancouver. Courtroom interior.

New Courthouse, Vancouver. View from South. Opposite: view over third floor pool to old courthouse.

The dramatic feature of the design, however, is an arrangement of elbow frames reaching up vertically at the edge of the stairs out of green planters and disappearing in their horizontal portions to become roof beams of the courtrooms, each of which are two storeys high. Erickson's roof arrangements always contain more than I can absorb at first glance; a second look revealed V-shaped steel supporting arms to the steel pipe space-frame of the roof, at the visible end of these extraordinary elbow frames.

"My office gives everything wonderful names," Erickson broke in suddenly. "They call those bent beam columns 'knees,' and the concrete boxes attached that are filled with green plants are 'flying planters.' All three sets of knees, from the level we are on to the roof top, were carefully planned to be identical. I don't want anything to interrupt their repetition." He hesitated. "I don't think I should tell you this, it sounds so odd, but I got the idea for them from the lemon groves in southern Italy, where whole slopes have an endless series of piers and trellises to shade the lemon trees."

We climbed the grand stairs to the next level, Erickson pointing out as we did so that the linear pattern of the beige ribbed carpet we were walking on had been specially dyed and woven to blend with the surrounding concrete. "I have also used fir as wood slatting all through the project to blur things, and because it's warm against the concrete," he said.

Originally, there was to have been an eighth floor and thirty-nine courtrooms, but government intervention had

110

eliminated one floor and reduced the courtrooms to thirty-five. On the balcony of the level we were on, we stopped to look at a freestanding lattice wood screen of American brown elm that hid the entrance to the courtroom. "I think these screens give a warmer look, but they were really difficult to put up," Erickson remarked, and while I was looking at the screen he disappeared through the door. I hastily followed and found Erickson already seated in a large courtroom, in a comfortable tan leather chair along a tan velvet wall, facing the raised judge's bench and the court space beneath it, which had a crimson carpet whose colour was repeated in the row of chairs in the jury box along the other wall.

I liked the warm red contrasting with soft tans that surrounded us in wood, walls, chairs and the carpet beneath our own feet. "I had some resistance from the judges," Erickson continued. "They wanted dark wood. They thought light wood too modern and not rich enough. My aim was to keep everything as quiet as possible."

The only daylight appeared to be coming in from skylights slanting towards the ceiling at the very top of the wall, and despite the handsome coffered lights in the concrete ceiling, I said I felt somewhat closed in. Erickson sighed, in what I now recognized as the sigh of some minor defeat. "I know," he said. "I wanted the courtrooms more open to the public, but it was the judges' choice to have a solid wall on the pedestrian hall side, for security. Notice the horizontals going across: the brass rail around the court officials' space; the judge's long bench; the cornice behind

him on the wall to give him extra dignity."

We took an elevator, handsomely finished in wood, to the top level, wandering through courtrooms similar except for size, all with white-walled retiring rooms behind for the juries, well furnished holding rooms for prisoners, and chambers for the judges. Then we walked down the stairs, stopping at each level to admire the vista of the pedestrian mall that can contain six hundred people, far below. In one of these pauses Erickson said, "I think we've come close to achieving what we wanted. With that space-frame embracing all the courts, you come out here and feel there *is* no barrier.

"We're very proud of our ventilating system in this building," Erickson said, as we continued down the stairs. "Cooling is a more serious problem here than heating, and we do two things. We cool the air by stack action—that is, we have vents that open at the bottom and top of the courthouse, like a greenhouse. The hot air rises and escapes at the top, and the cooler air is brought in from the bottom; in between, the air in motion has a comforting effect on your skin. Second, as the trees inside that you see below us grow larger, they will give more shade for people to sit under. We have a mixture of orange, grapefruit and tangerine trees here."

At the first gallery level we turned right and came to a glassed-in restaurant area. We were looking over a glistening rectangle of water on the roof-top of the visiting provincial officials' quarters directly at the old courthouse as if nothing intervened. "The dome of the old courthouse that you see here

reflected in the pool always strikes me as slightly Byzantine," Erickson said. "This was sighted to give you just that view. The old, seen through the new. This is my favourite place. Tall buildings eventually will be all around this and that's what it needs. Then it will look like the centre of a walled city."

We left, riding down in an elevator to the street where Erickson had parked the car. He said, "When we started, the judges' committee told us they preferred a classical courthouse for its dignity. But by working closely with them —allowing them to be part of the design process—they became our greatest supporters in this drastically different courthouse. It proved to me that the most conservative citizens can be most creative and courageous, given the opportunity."

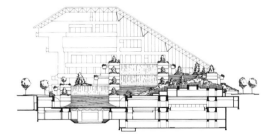

W e got in the car and started off for the Museum of Anthropology on the U.B.C. campus.

"When you design a museum, the important thing is to ask questions about the real nature of the institution," Erickson said as he drove carefully through residential Vancouver in late-afternoon traffic. "Otherwise, you get a dull place where some things are displayed, the public pays entrance fees, and nine-tenths of the museum's contents are in storage. Most museums are just collecting. If that's all a museum can be, I'm not interested. So you ask, 'How can it make a valid contribution to our lives?' My thinking on the importance of the museum in giving one a sense of pride in one's own culture was crystallized by a black man, Jim Woods, whom I met at a conference on cities at the University of Illinois. He had started the Studio Watts Workshop in Los Angeles during the riots. He told me that in the museums he visited as a child he had discovered the wonder of human achievement and the great art of his own forebears. Northwest Coast Indian culture is the chief collection of the U.B.C. Museum of Anthropology, and the main problem of our native population, the Northwest Coast Indians, is that the white people took away their dignity by destroying their culture and beliefs and offered nothing but welfare in return. The museum should reassure our Indians of the greatness of their culture, and perhaps give them back some of their dignity and confidence, which was taken away by conquest, and then, more humiliatingly, later, by welfare."

We were now on the university grounds, heading down a broad avenue toward a sprawling set of buildings. "In

Museum of Anthropology, University of British Columbia, Vancouver (1972)

"I wanted everything in greys; sun and salt-bleached wood that is a silvered colour; a grey carpet to join with the pebbles outside; and concrete that is like pebbles and sympathetic to the colour of the wood. A very quick natural background. Then you see the objects."
—Erickson

Top: side view from south. Bottom: Rear view from east. Opposite: interior of great hall.

most museums, the lectures and written labels bore me, and I feel cheated by the contents being chiefly in storage," Erickson said. "The concept of visible storage—of having the storerooms open to the public—arose when I was talking with the two people who developed the university's Northwest Coast Indian collection over the past thirty years: Audrey Hawthorn, the curator of the previous so-called museum, which had a couple of rooms in the basement of the university library; and her husband, Harry, who was the head of the Department of Anthropology and Sociology. Both are now retired. In our museum, if you become fascinated by Indian rattles or horn spoons you can follow your curiosity into the storage area and see all the objects related to them. Everything."

It was just after visiting hours, and the museum entrance, a great carved-wood box with panels that opened as doors, was locked. Entering through the back of the building, we came to the storage area first. When Erickson ran his hand down two panels of electric wall switches and the lights went on, I was facing huge glass cases that held what appeared to be a helter-skelter assortment of objects. The sight had the fascination of a gigantic junk shop. I was drawn to a case containing some magnificent Haida masks—dramatic, sombre carvings like nothing I had ever seen before. "Your superconscious finding what's relevant to you," Erickson said, smiling. "Here the whole mess, good and bad, gives you the opportunity to train your eye and teach yourself, which is the only way to learn. It's wrong for anyone to assume he can teach

114

anyone else. I myself was teaching selfishly, to learn as much as I could—discovering what I was talking about while I lectured."

We went over to a high chest of drawers, and he urged me to look inside. I pulled out a flat drawer and found Indian jewelry, arranged so I could see everything, under a locked Plexiglas cover.

We walked through a closed corridor with concrete walls on both sides which led to the main entrance, and now we were standing just inside the doors, at the head of a broad carpeted ramp the colour of a sandy beach. We started slowly down this long aisle, which had great carved figures of beaked birds and awesome woodland animals, crouched or stalking, on either side, and totem poles, mysterious and marvellous in the fading light: the relics of an ancient culture for which North America had been home long before my ancestors arrived—a world I was seeing for the first time.

"You have to get inside the minds of the people who made these primitive sculptures, the masks, the totem poles," Erickson said quietly. "You have to have experienced their fears and superstitions concerning their rain forest and their coastal mountains. In a logging camp I worked in as a boy, I took long walks in the wilderness and knew the terror of being lost, and felt how the forest becomes alive and threatening. Like the Japanese, the Indians here worshipped every aspect of nature, chanting to the trees to forgive them when they stripped bark for baskets, singing to the fish for forgiveness, apologizing for human transgressions

against nature. When I was designing the museum, I remembered a photograph of an early Indian village between the edge of the forest and the edge of the sea. The inhabitants had carved the trees with the animals they hunted and the fish they netted, and arranged these marvellous totems that gave special powers to the families who owned them in a legend of natural survival, following the crescent of the beach."

We had been moving slowly down the ramp. Suddenly, the sky burst open around us: we were in a glass hall of dazzling proportions, facing snow-covered mountains across Howe Sound, an arm of the Pacific. Silvery-yellow light from the setting sun streamed out from behind a black cloud and played on the brooding, weather-beaten carved profiles of totems.

I looked up, expecting open sky, and saw a succession of skylights framed in concrete, the supporting posts progressively changing proportions from wide and low, where we were standing, to a height of fifty feet at the far end. These were not sloping and conventional flat skylights but Plexiglas in long, vaulted curves that disappeared into the sky, so that I had to look twice to see that anything was there. The glass walls of the great hall had been hung from the ceiling in panels joined by bronze plates, each about four by five inches, in a lovely, light pattern that enhanced the dignity and magnificence of the carvings.

I was bewitched.

"I am really pleased with this room," I heard Erickson say, as if from far away. "I am infuriated with my buildings that

don't come off, but I really enjoy the ones that do."

I turned and looked at him. He appeared slight and small in this lofty space, standing with his hands buried in the pockets of his trenchcoat, its collar turned up. His long face and long, pointed nose melded into the beaked profile of the bird on the carving behind his shoulder.

"I insisted that the totem poles look outward, not at you: off into the distance," Erickson said suddenly. "One of the great mysteries of the caryatids on the Acropolis is that they do not look at you. Or at anything."

I raised my eyes to the Plexiglas and concrete ceiling, and, following my gaze, he said, "That long horizontal beam is one hundred and eighty feet, and I was told that such a long beam was technically impossible, but there is always a contest over how much can be realized. I didn't do it consciously, but in the succession of frames—from low and wide to narrow and tall posts and beams—that enclose this room, each echoes the form of the frame of an Indian house."

We walked on, to the glass wall at the end, facing the mountains and the sea. Directly outside, there was an irregular pebbled area edged with a big mound of earth. To the left were two log houses—a large and a small one—and on the right were two painted totem poles. "The idea that came to me first was an ethnobotanical outdoor museum," Erickson said. "Most of my concepts have to do with how one moves, and since the site is sloped I felt that the whole movement should be down a long ramp, with more and more revealed, until the whole space burst open with a view of the sea. The log houses are both Haida and the totems are Kwakiutl, and we plan to add a Kwakiutl house as well. That pebbled area will be filled with water, and will appear to extend to the sea. It will look as if it were a typical village setting on an inlet, and from here the Tantalus Mountains you see will be reflected in the water. The lake and these outdoor buildings are on the earthquake line of this embankment, and all my plans, which include indigenous plantings, aim to help stop the erosion, although the university doesn't quite see it that way, yet. I'll leave the space filled with pebbles until I get what I want.''

Erickson did not seem in a hurry to leave. "Each year, when I go on one of my journeys, I discover something important to my understanding of my work, my values, and my life," he said. "Some years ago, I returned to paradise —to Bali. I visited a remote village consisting of one wide street. Down its centre ran a series of beautiful pavilions, each with a ritual function—one for old men, one for women, one for children, and so on—where the folklore was handed down and the culture was perpetuated. On either side were the houses where the families were born, grew up, and died. I visited one of the houses, with a courtyard, a household shrine, a room for musical instruments and masks (because everyone takes part in music and dancing), a kitchen, a shrine for the kitchen, rooms for the family, for the newly married couples, even a room for birth and a room for dying. What impressed me was that the house not only proved useful for living

Museum of Anthropology. Visual Storage.

Museum of Anthropology. Koerner gallery.

Overleaf: view from east at night.

but celebrated all the basic events of
life; and in the centre was the beginning
and the end. The continuity made an
extraordinary impression on me. My
question to myself is 'How can I put
that same strength of meaning, that
profound symbol of existence, into
whatever I build?'" He turned to leave.
"It may take years for me to absorb and
translate this. It has to go into my
superconscious first."

INDEX

Note: Bold page numbers refer to illustrations or captions.